11+ Non-verbal Reasoning

WORKBOOK 2

Non-verbal Reasoning Technique

Dr Stephen C Curran
with Andrea Richardson
Edited by Dr Tandip Singh Mann

This book belongs to

ae TUITION

Accelerated Education Publications Ltd

Contents

6. Components   Pages
1. Key Questions in NVR   3
2. Elimination Skills   3
3. Descriptive Skills   3-4

7. Odd One Out
1. Basic Level   5-7
2. Advanced Level   8-10

8. Codes
1. Type 1 - Level Two   11-13
2. Type 2 - Level Two   14-16
3. Type 1 - Level Three   17-19
4. Type 1 - Level Four   20-22

9. Analogies
1. Level One   23-25
2. Level Two   26-28
3. Level Three   29-31
4. Levels Four & Five   32-34

10. Similarities
1. Level One   35-37
2. Level Two   38-40
3. Level Three   41-43
4. Levels Four & Five   44-46

11. Series   Pages
1. Level One   47-49
2. Level Two   50-52
3. Level Three   53-55
4. Levels Four & Five   56-58

12. Matrices
1. Level One   59-61
2. Level Two   62-64
3. Level Three   65-67
4. Levels Four & Five   68-70

13. Revision
1. Odd One Out   71
2. Codes   72
3. Analogy   73
4. Similarities   74
5. Series   75
6. Matrices   76

© 2006 Stephen Curran

Chapter Six
COMPONENTS

The **Components** of Non-verbal Reasoning comprise:
Key Questions • Elimination Skills • Descriptive Skills

1. Key Questions in NVR

All NVR questions are centred around three key areas:
1) The shape most **Similar** 2) The shape most **Different**
3) The next shape in a **Series** of shapes (identify a pattern).

2. Elimination Skills

Eliminating the wrong options one by one, by marking them or crossing them out, helps to identify the answer.

Example: Which shape is most like the Test Shape?

Test Shape

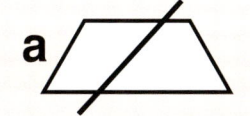

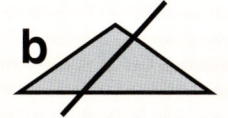

Answer: **d** - It is four-sided and has a Grey Fill.

3. Descriptive Skills

Descriptive Skills in Non-verbal Reasoning aid understanding. A summary of descriptive skills is given below:
Elements • Movements • Manipulations • Patterns • Layering

a. Elements
(i) Shapes

Standard Shapes comprise all 'closed' geometrically defined shapes.   **Rectangle**

Specialist Shapes comprise everyday recognisable 'closed' shapes.   **Boat**

© 2006 Stephen Curran

(ii) Fills

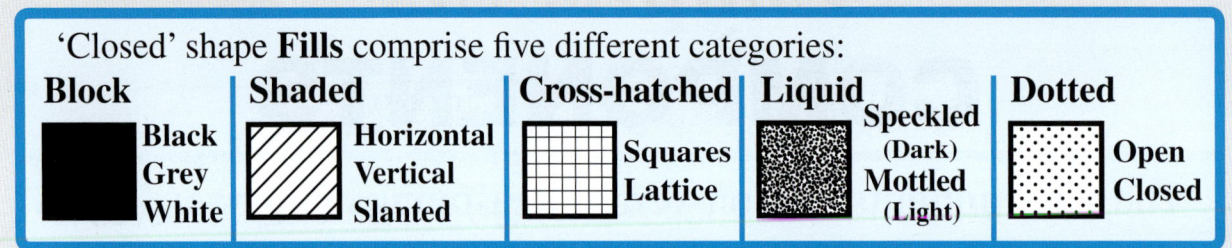

'Closed' shape **Fills** comprise five different categories:

Block	Shaded	Cross-hatched	Liquid	Dotted
Black / Grey / White	Horizontal / Vertical / Slanted	Squares / Lattice	Speckled (Dark) / Mottled (Light)	Open / Closed

(iii) Lines

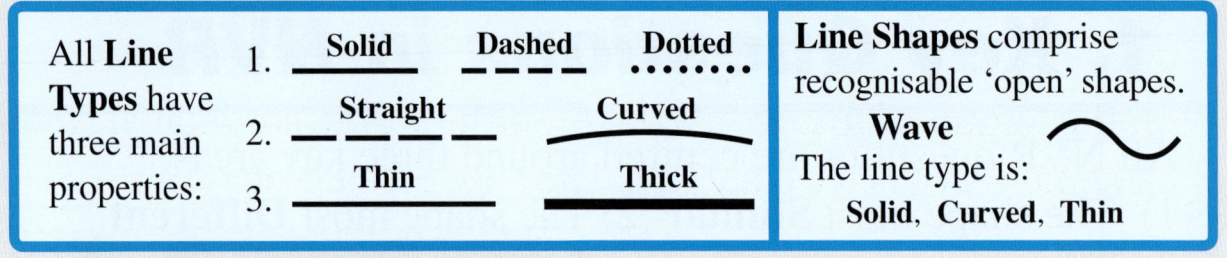

All **Line Types** have three main properties:
1. Solid, Dashed, Dotted
2. Straight, Curved
3. Thin, Thick

Line Shapes comprise recognisable 'open' shapes.

Wave — The line type is: Solid, Curved, Thin

b. Movements

In Non-verbal Reasoning, shapes can **Move** in five different ways:

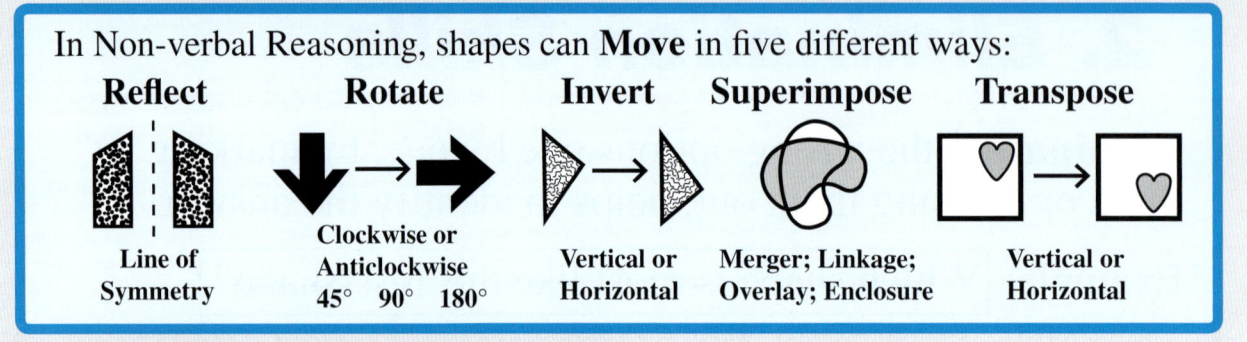

- **Reflect** — Line of Symmetry
- **Rotate** — Clockwise or Anticlockwise 45° 90° 180°
- **Invert** — Vertical or Horizontal
- **Superimpose** — Merger; Linkage; Overlay; Enclosure
- **Transpose** — Vertical or Horizontal

c. Manipulations

In Non-verbal Reasoning, shapes can be **Manipulated** in the following five ways:

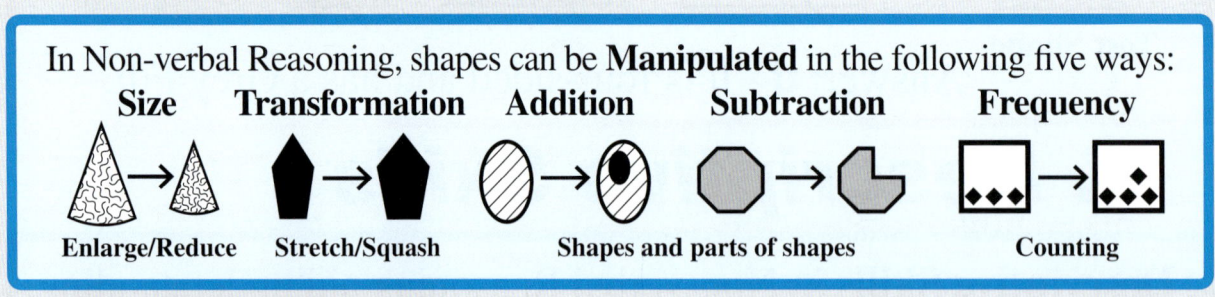

- **Size** — Enlarge/Reduce
- **Transformation** — Stretch/Squash
- **Addition** — Shapes and parts of shapes
- **Subtraction** — Shapes and parts of shapes
- **Frequency** — Counting

d. Patterns

In Non-verbal Reasoning, shapes can make **Patterns** in two different ways:

Repetition   **Cumulation**

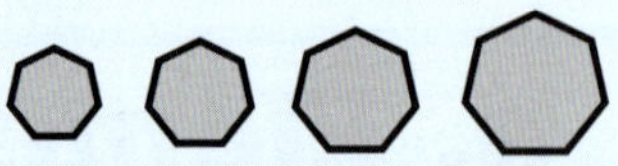

e. Layering

Layering occurs when changes to shapes or figures are combined. Questions with up to five layers or changes can seem complex. **This book involves learning to identify & describe these layers.**

© 2006 Stephen Curran

Chapter Seven
ODD ONE OUT

In Verbal Reasoning, choosing the **Odd One Out** involves seeing how the meaning of each word in a group of words relates to the other words.

Example:

In this group of five words, three of the words are related in some way and two are not. They are the odd ones out.

<u>ash</u>   **branch**   <u>oak</u>   **leaf**   <u>willow</u>

branch and **leaf** are odd ones out as they are not tree types.

In Non-verbal Reasoning, choosing the odd one out involves spotting which likeness links a group of shapes and identifying which shape does not have this likeness.

Example:

All the shapes have four sides except the Triangle which only has three sides, so this is the odd one out.

1. Basic Level

Odd one out questions only ever operate at Level One. This means there is only one layer or change to look for. On easier questions we can spot this very quickly.

Example: Which shape is most unlike the others?

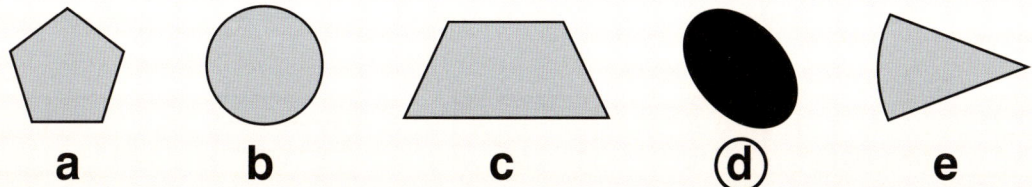

a   b   c   ⓓ   e

Answer: **d**

All the shapes have a Grey Fill except the Ellipse, which has a Black Fill, making it the odd one out.

© 2006 Stephen Curran

Exercise 7: 1
Which shape or figure is the odd one out?

1)

a   b   c   d   e

Why? _The Triangle is smaller than the other Triangles._

Answer ____

2)

a   b   c   d   e

Why? _____

Answer ____

3)

a   b   c   d   e

Why? _____

Answer ____

4)

a   b   c   d   e

Why? _____

Answer ____

5)

a   b   c   d   e

Why? _____

Answer ____

© 2006 Stephen Curran

6)

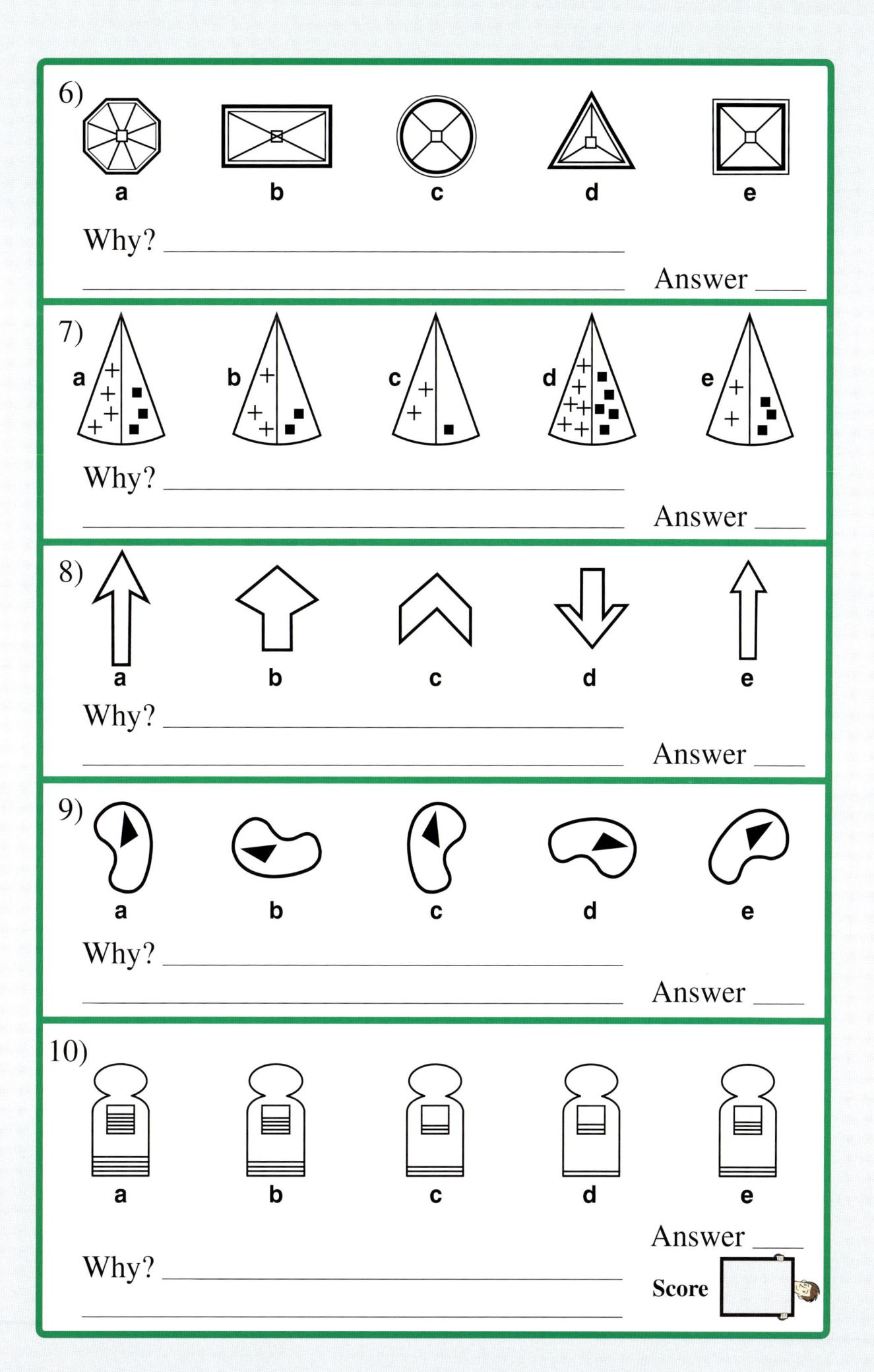

a   b   c   d   e

Why? _____

_____ Answer ____

7)

a   b   c   d   e

Why? _____

_____ Answer ____

8)

a   b   c   d   e

Why? _____

_____ Answer ____

9)

a   b   c   d   e

Why? _____

_____ Answer ____

10)

a   b   c   d   e

Answer ____

Why? _____

_____ Score ____

© 2006 Stephen Curran

2. Advanced Level

Although odd one out questions only ever operate at Level One (one major difference), it is best to solve more difficult questions by eliminating all the misleading options first. In other words, we do the question in reverse.

Example: Which figure is most unlike the others?

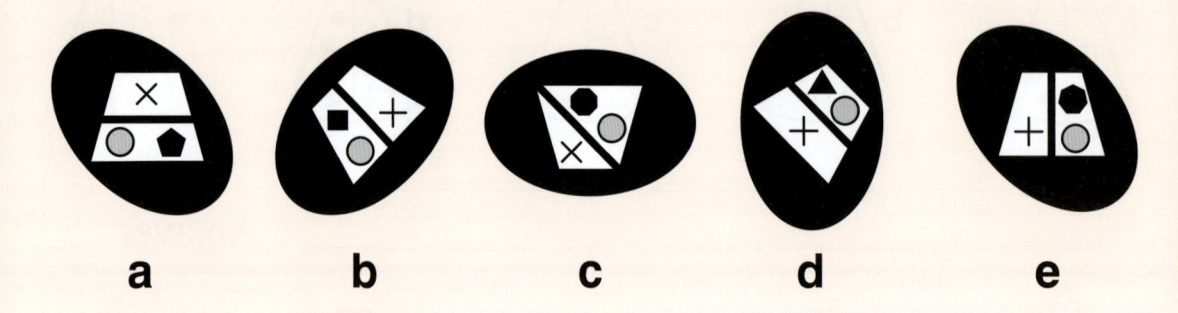

a   b   c   d   e

Elimination Process

By comparing the figures we eliminate the following:

1. The Black Filled Ellipse points in all four directions (vertically, horizontally, diagonally left and diagonally right).

2. The White Filled enclosed Trapezium points in all four directions (upright, facing down, diagonally left and diagonally right).

3. Two Trapezium Shapes enclose a Cross Shape (like a multiplication sign) and three enclose a Cross Shape (like an addition sign). These shapes are always on their own in one half.

4. All the Trapezium Shapes enclose a Circle with a Grey Fill.

5. All the Trapezium Shapes enclose a different Regular Polygon with a Black Fill.

Final Observation and Choice

All the Trapezium Shapes have a Line drawn across them, but in only one does this Line go to the vertices or corners of the Trapezium.

Answer: **c**

Exercise 7: 2

Which shape or figure is the odd one out?

1)

    a   b   c   d   e

Why? *The two Segment Shapes inside the Circle are different from those in the other Circles.*

Answer ____

2)

    a   b   c   d   e

Why? _____

_____ Answer ____

3)

    a   b   c   d   e

Why? _____

_____ Answer ____

4)

    a   b   c   d   e

Why? _____

_____ Answer ____

5)

    a   b   c   d   e

Why? _____

_____ Answer ____

© 2006 Stephen Curran

6) a b c d e

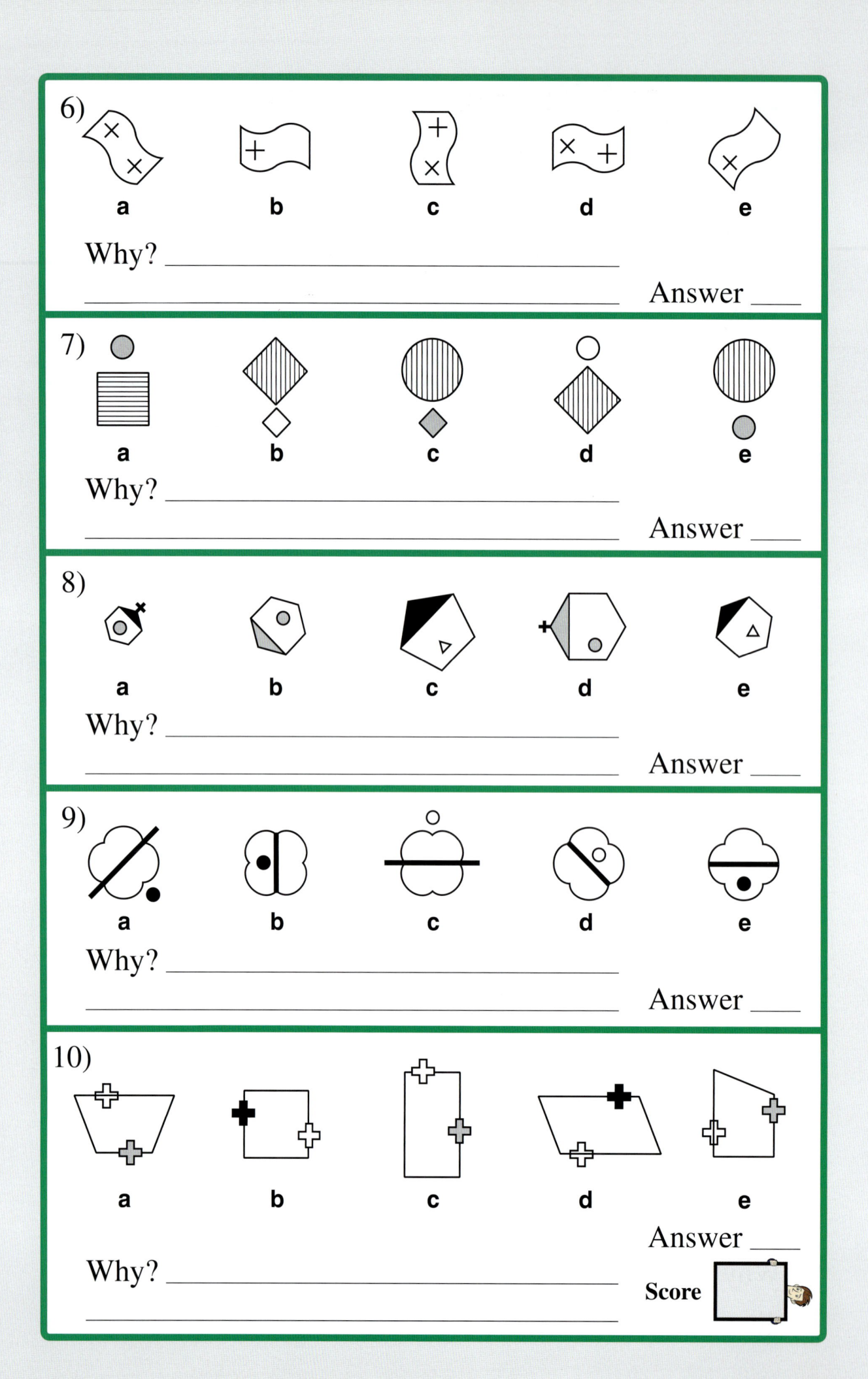

Why? _____

_____ Answer ____

7) a b c d e

Why? _____

_____ Answer ____

8) a b c d e

Why? _____

_____ Answer ____

9) a b c d e

Why? _____

_____ Answer ____

10) a b c d e

Answer ____

Why? _____

_____ Score ____

Chapter Eight
CODES

The skill of **Decoding** in Verbal Reasoning involves finding out what the letters or numbers represent.

For example: If **678** means **PIT**, what does **876** mean?

Each digit represents a letter. Answer: **TIP**

In Non-verbal Reasoning, letters are often used to represent:

Shapes • **Fills** • **Lines**

1. Type 1 - Level Two

Decoding in Non-verbal Reasoning involves working out which letters go with which shapes. A **Level Two** code question has two letters which represent the correct shape. Level One (one letter) questions are too easy for tests.

Example: Which pair of letters represents the Test Shape?

| MA
| MB   ■   NB   MB   MC   AM   NA
| Test Shape   a   b   c   d   e
| ▲ NC

The Code Rules are as follows:

Layer One - **M** stands for Squares; **N** stands for Triangles.
Layer Two - **A** stands for a White Fill; **B** for a Grey Fill; **C** for a Black Fill.

~~NB~~   ~~MB~~   MC   ~~AM~~   ~~NA~~
 a   b   c   d   e

It is important to **eliminate** the wrong possibilities:

a and **e** - **NB** and **NA** are incorrect because they stand for Triangles.
b - **MB** is incorrect because **B** stands for a Grey Fill.
d - **AM** is incorrect because **A** stands for a White Fill and the letters are not in the correct order, which is not permitted.

Answer: **c** - **M** stands for Square; **C** stands for a Black Fill.

Exercise 8: 1

Which pair of letters on the right represents the Test Shape or Figure?

1)

RL
RJ
QJ

Test Shape

QK	QL	RK	JR	JQ
a	b	c	d	e

Code Rules:
i) R - Small Squares; Q - Large Squares.
ii) L - Right Slant Shaded Fill; J - Lattice Fill.

Answer ____

2)

MA
MB
NA

Test Figure

AN	MA	NB	AM	MN
a	b	c	d	e

Code Rules:
i) _____
ii) _____

Answer ____

3)

TG
SF
SG

Test Shape

SH	SG	TS	TG	TF
a	b	c	d	e

Code Rules:
i) _____
ii) _____

Answer ____

4)

XB
YA
XA

Test Shape

YB	BX	AX	YA	AB
a	b	c	d	e

Code Rules:
i) _____
ii) _____

Answer ____

5)

QC
PC
PD

Test Shape

QP	DQ	QD	PC	CD
a	b	c	d	e

Code Rules:
i) _____
ii) _____

Answer ____

12   © 2006 Stephen Curran

6)

JW
KX
LX

Test Figure

JX KW WX LW XK
a   b   c   d   e

Code Rules:
i) _____
ii) _____

Answer ____

7)

AN
BO
CN

Test Shape

AO NO NC CO BN
a   b   c   d   e

Code Rules:
i) _____
ii) _____

Answer ____

8)

RF
SG
TG
SF

Test Figure

FS SG RG TF RS
a   b   c   d   e

Code Rules:
i) _____
ii) _____

Answer ____

9)

FL
GM
FN

Test Figure

GL MN GN FM LF
a   b   c   d   e

Code Rules:
i) _____
ii) _____

Answer ____

10)

WA
XB
YB
ZA

Test Figure

XA WB YA ZB XY
a   b   c   d   e

Code Rules:
i) _____
ii) _____

Answer ____

Score ____

© 2006 Stephen Curran

2. Type 2 - Level Two

Type 2 code questions look different but work in the same way as Type 1. This type only ever has two letters, so it always functions as a Level Two question.

Example: Which two letters represent the Test Figure?

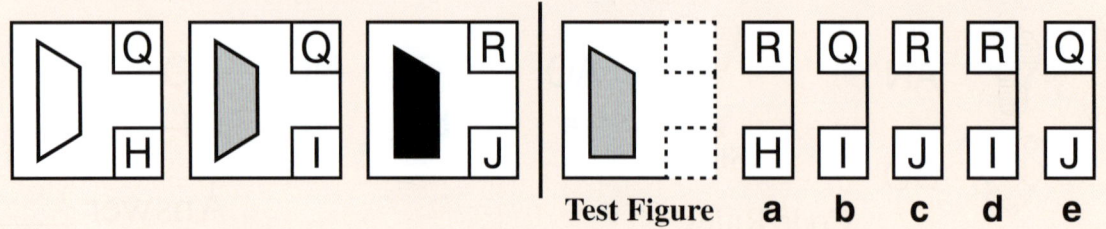

The Code Rules are as follows:

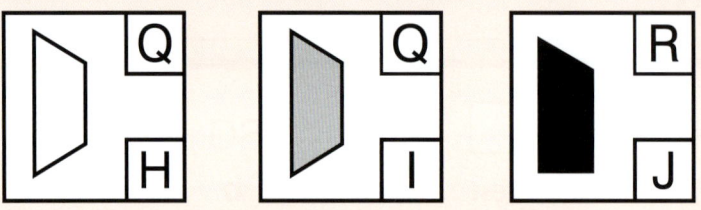

Layer One - **Q** stands for an Isosceles Trapezium;
R stands for an ordinary Trapezium.
Layer Two - **H** stands for a White Fill; **I** for a Grey Fill; **J** for a Black Fill.

The Set of Codes:

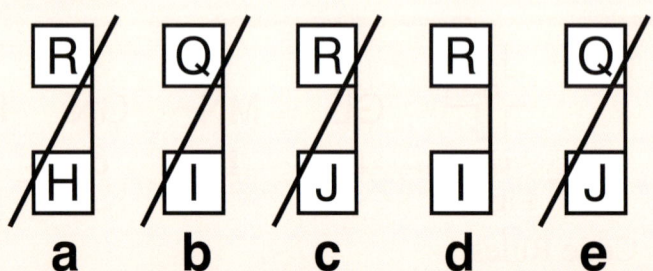

It is important to **eliminate** the wrong possibilities:
b and **e** - **QI** and **QJ** are incorrect because they stand for the wrong shape.
a - **RH** is incorrect because **H** stands for a White Fill.
c - **RJ** is incorrect because **J** stands for a Black Fill.

The Test Shape and the Correct Code:

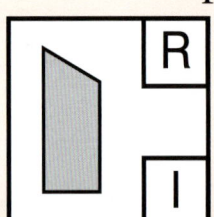

Layer One
R stands for an ordinary Trapezium.
Layer Two
I stands for a Grey Fill.

Answer: **d** - **RI** is the correct code.

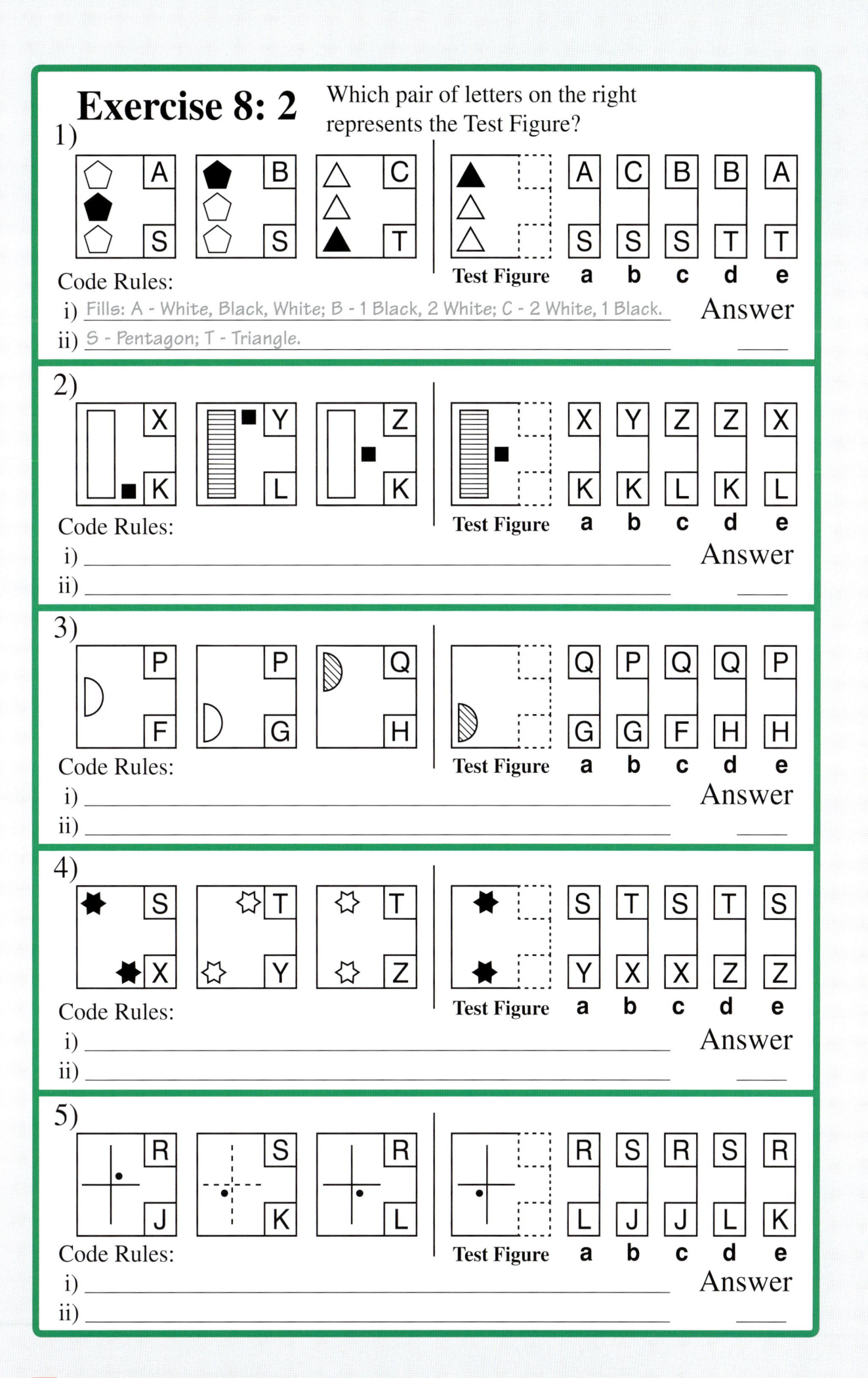

Exercise 8: 2

Which pair of letters on the right represents the Test Figure?

1)

Code Rules:
i) Fills: A - White, Black, White; B - 1 Black, 2 White; C - 2 White, 1 Black.
ii) S - Pentagon; T - Triangle.

Answer ____

2)

Code Rules:
i) ____
ii) ____

Answer ____

3)

Code Rules:
i) ____
ii) ____

Answer ____

4)

Code Rules:
i) ____
ii) ____

Answer ____

5)

Code Rules:
i) ____
ii) ____

Answer ____

© 2006 Stephen Curran

6)

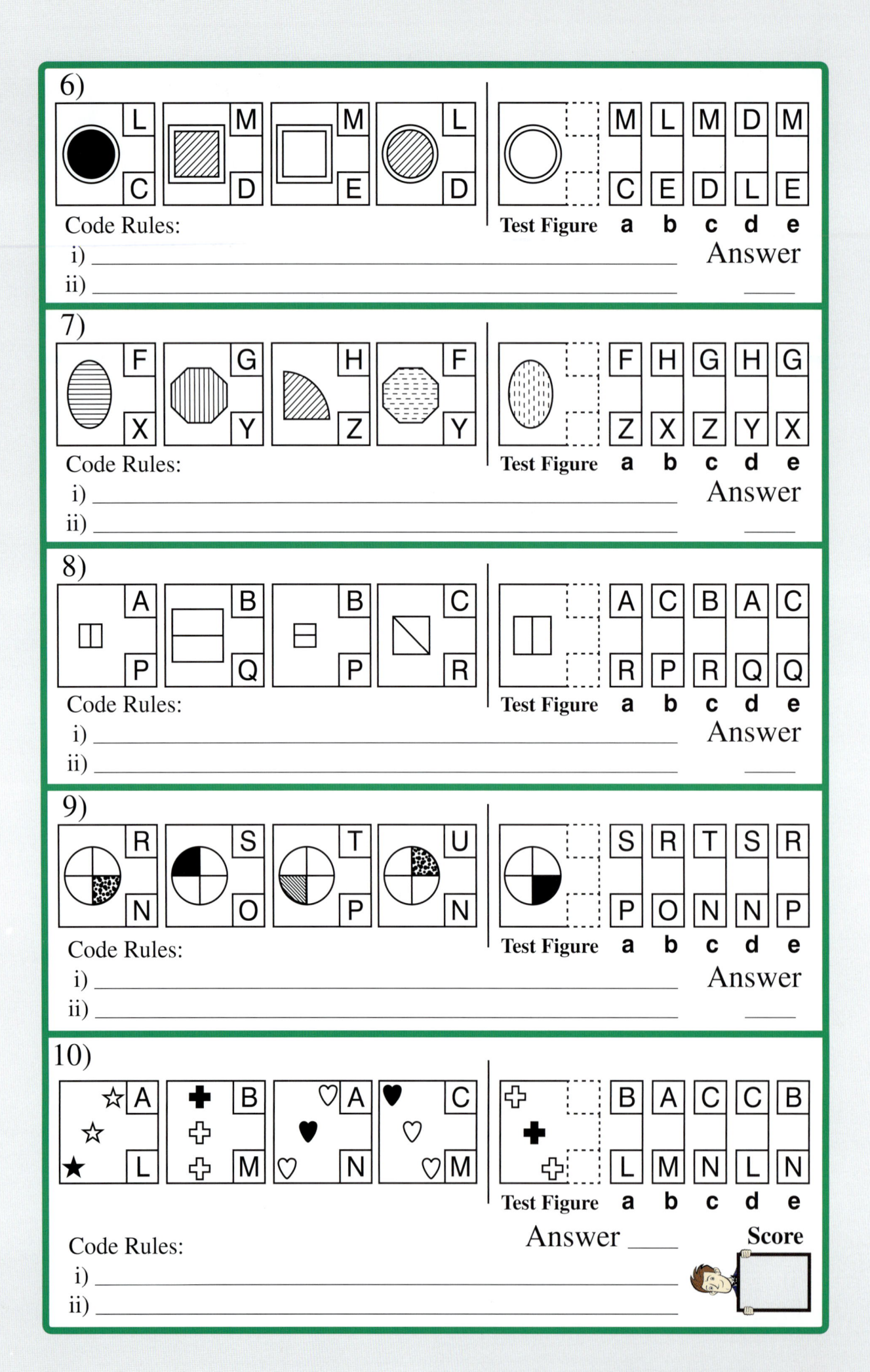

Code Rules:
i) _____
ii) _____

Test Figure   a b c d e
Answer ____

7)

Code Rules:
i) _____
ii) _____

Test Figure   a b c d e
Answer ____

8)

Code Rules:
i) _____
ii) _____

Test Figure   a b c d e
Answer ____

9)

Code Rules:
i) _____
ii) _____

Test Figure   a b c d e
Answer ____

10)

Code Rules:
i) _____
ii) _____

Test Figure   a b c d e
Answer ____   Score

3. Type 1 - Level Three

A **Level Three** code question has three letters which represent the correct shape.

Example: Which three letters represent the Test Figure?

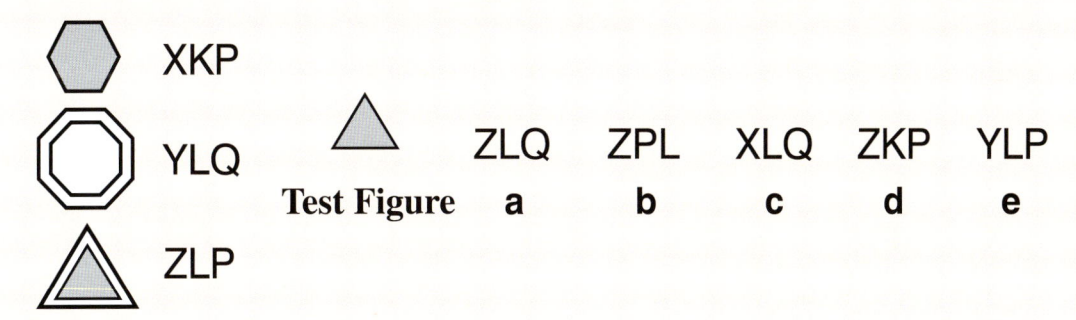

XKP

YLQ   ZLQ   ZPL   XLQ   ZKP   YLP

Test Figure   **a**   **b**   **c**   **d**   **e**

ZLP

The Code Rules are as follows:

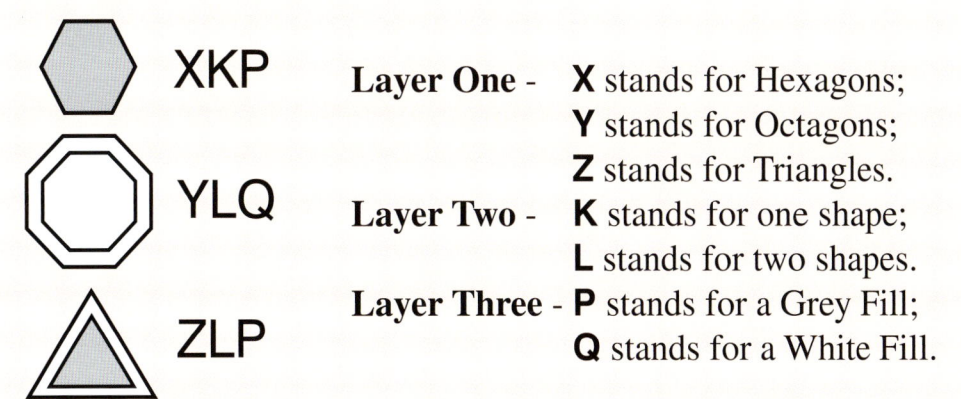

XKP   **Layer One -**   **X** stands for Hexagons;
                             Y stands for Octagons;
                             Z stands for Triangles.

YLQ   **Layer Two -**   **K** stands for one shape;
                             L stands for two shapes.

ZLP   **Layer Three -**   **P** stands for a Grey Fill;
                                Q stands for a White Fill.

The Set of Codes:

~~ZLQ~~   ~~ZPL~~   ~~XLQ~~   ZKP   ~~YLP~~

a   **b**   **c**   **d**   **e**

It is important to **eliminate** the wrong possibilities:
c and **e** - **XLQ** and **YLP** are incorrect as they stand for the wrong shapes.
a - **ZLQ** is incorrect because **L** stands for two shapes and **Q** stands for shapes with a White Fill.
b - **ZPL** is incorrect because **L** stands for two shapes. The letters are also in the wrong order which is not permitted.

The Test Shape and the Correct Code:

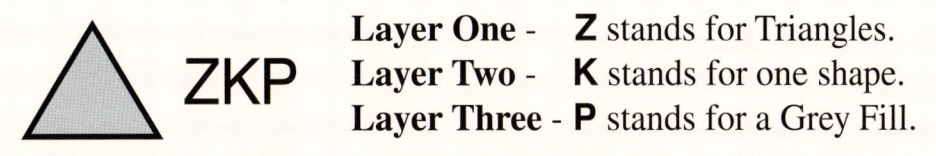

ZKP   **Layer One -**   **Z** stands for Triangles.
           Layer Two -   **K** stands for one shape.
           Layer Three -   **P** stands for a Grey Fill.

Answer: **d** - **ZKP** is the correct code.

© 2006 Stephen Curran

Exercise 8: 3

Which three letters on the right represent the Test Figure?

1) RMA
   RNB
   SNC

   Test Figure | SNA | RMB | SMA | RNC | RNA
   | a | b | c | d | e

   Code Rules:
   i) R - Large Ellipse; S - Small Ellipse.
   ii) Enclosed Ellipse: M - White Fill; N - Black Fill.
   iii) Large Ellipse: A - White Fill; B - Vertical Fill; C - Horizontal Fill.

   Answer ____

2) ALS
   AMT
   BMS

   Test Figure | ALT | BMT | BLS | AMS | BLT
   | a | b | c | d | e

   Code Rules:
   i) _____
   ii) _____
   iii) _____

   Answer ____

3) XKP
   XLR
   YLP

   Test Figure | YKP | XKL | XLP | YLR | YKR
   | a | b | c | d | e

   Code Rules:
   i) _____
   ii) _____
   iii) _____

   Answer ____

4) GYR
   HYS
   HZR

   Test Figure | HYR | HZS | GZS | GYS | GZR
   | a | b | c | d | e

   Code Rules:
   i) _____
   ii) _____
   iii) _____

   Answer ____

5) WMJ
   XNJ
   XMK

   Test Figure | XNK | XMJ | WNK | WMK | WNJ
   | a | b | c | d | e

   Code Rules:
   i) _____
   ii) _____
   iii) _____

   Answer ____

© 2006 Stephen Curran

6) QGA
RFA
SGB

Test Figure

RGA	QFA	FGB	RFB	QFB
a	b	c	d	e

Code Rules:
i) _____
ii) _____
iii) _____

Answer ____

7) LQY
LPZ
MOY

Test Figure

LQZ	MQY	LOZ	LPY	MQZ
a	b	c	d	e

Code Rules:
i) _____
ii) _____
iii) _____

Answer ____

8) TAQ
UBQ
VAR
TCQ

Test Figure

TBQ	UCR	VCQ	UAR	VBQ
a	b	c	d	e

Code Rules:
i) _____
ii) _____
iii) _____

Answer ____

9) GLA
HMA
GMB

Test Figure

GMA	GLB	HLB	HMB	HLA
a	b	c	d	e

Code Rules:
i) _____
ii) _____
iii) _____

Answer ____

10) JQY
KPY
JPZ

Test Figure

KQZ	JQZ	KQY	JPY	KPZ
a	b	c	d	e

Code Rules:
i) _____
ii) _____
iii) _____

Answer ____

Score ____

© 2006 Stephen Curran

4. Type 1 - Level Four

A **Level Four** code question has four letters which represent the correct figure.

Example: Which four letters represent the Test Figure?

AMJX

BNKX

BMJY BMJX CNKY ANJX ANKY
Test Figure   a   b   c   d   e

CNJY

The Code Rules are as follows:

AMJX   Layer One - **A** stands for Heart Shapes;
       B stands for Bone Shapes;
       C stands for Triangles.

BNKX   Layer Two - **M** stands for an enclosure;
       N stands for an overlay.

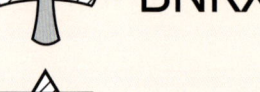

       Layer Three - **J** stands for a White Fill;
       K stands for a Grey Fill.

CNJY   Layer Four - **X** stands for a Black Fill Circle;
       Y stands for a White Fill Circle.

The Set of Codes:

~~BMJY~~ ~~BMJX~~ ~~CNKY~~ ~~ANJX~~ ANKY
  a   b   c   d   e

It is important to **eliminate** the wrong possibilities:

b and **c** - **BMJX** and **CNKY** are incorrect as they stand for the wrong shapes.
a - **BMJY** is incorrect because **M** stands for an enclosure and **J** stands for a White Fill.
d - **ANJX** is incorrect because **X** stands for a Black Fill Circle.

The Test Shape and the Correct Code:

ANKY   Layer One -   **A** stands for Heart Shapes.
       Layer Two -   **N** stands for an overlay.
       Layer Three - **K** stands for a Grey Fill.
       Layer Four - **Y** stands for a White Fill Circle.

Answer: **e** - **ANKY** is the correct code.

© 2006 Stephen Curran

Exercise 8: 4

Which four letters on the right represent the given figure?

Score ☐

1) ↑ EMAP
   ⊡ ENBQ
   ⊢● FMCQ

   ←◻   EMBQ   FNAP   ENAP   FNAQ   ENCP
               a   b   c   d   e

   Code Rules: Answer ____
   i) E - Square; F - Circle.
   ii) M - Black Fill; N - White Fill.
   iii) A - Shape at bottom; B - Shape to left; C - Shape to right.
   iv) P - Arrow Ending; Q - Straight Ending.

2) ZLPC
   XMPD
   XLQE

   ZMPD   ZLPD   XLPE   ZLQD   XMQC
      a   b   c   d   e

   Code Rules: Answer ____
   i) _____
   ii) _____
   iii) _____
   iv) _____

3) XKPC
   XLQD
   YKRD

   XKRC   XLRC   YLQC   XLPC   YKQD
      a   b   c   d   e

   Code Rules: Answer ____
   i) _____
   ii) _____
   iii) _____
   iv) _____

4) GYRJ
   HYSK
   GZTK

   GZRK   HZSK   GYSJ   GZSJ   HYTJ
      a   b   c   d   e

   Code Rules: Answer ____
   i) _____
   ii) _____
   iii) _____
   iv) _____

5) WMJA
   XNKA
   WNLB

   XMLB   WMLB   XMKA   WNLA   XNJB
      a   b   c   d   e

   Code Rules: Answer ____
   i) _____
   ii) _____
   iii) _____
   iv) _____

© 2006 Stephen Curran

6) QGAW / RGBX / SHAX

QHBX (a) RHAX (b) SHBW (c) QGBX (d) QHAX (e)

Code Rules:
i) _____
ii) _____
iii) _____
iv) _____

Answer ____

7) LQXD / LPYE / KPZD

KQZD (a) LPZE (b) KPXD (c) KQZE (d) LQYE (e)

Code Rules:
i) _____
ii) _____
iii) _____
iv) _____

Answer ____

8) TAPY / UBQY / UARZ

TBRZ (a) UBPY (b) TAQZ (c) TBRY (d) UARZ (e)

Code Rules:
i) _____
ii) _____
iii) _____
iv) _____

Answer ____

9) JPFC / KPGD / KQHC

KQGD (a) JPFD (b) JQGC (c) KPHC (d) JQFD (e)

Code Rules:
i) _____
ii) _____
iii) _____
iv) _____

Answer ____

10) AFSY / BGSZ / AHTZ

AGTZ (a) BFTZ (b) BHSY (c) AFTZ (d) BGSY (e)

Code Rules:
i) _____
ii) _____
iii) _____
iv) _____

Answer ____

Chapter Nine
ANALOGIES

In Verbal Reasoning, an **Analogy** is a similarity in meaning between two parallel statements or words. This comparison is linked by the word '**as**' which means '**like**'.

For example: **Huge** is to **tiny** as **wide** is to **narrow**

In a Non-verbal Reasoning analogy question, a similarity can be established between two sets of shapes.

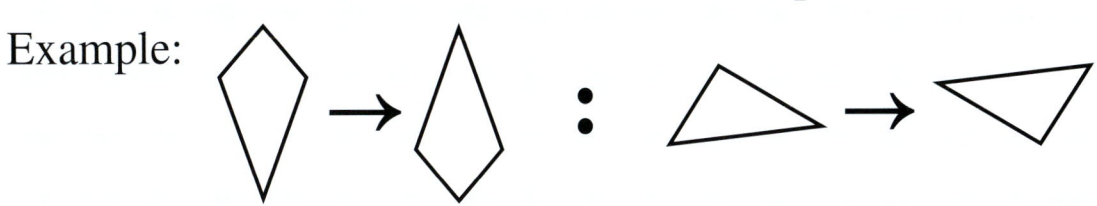

Example:

The first Kite has been rotated 180° to form the second Kite. The **Colon Symbol** (:) in between means '**as**' or '**like**'. Therefore the first Triangle must be rotated 180° to form the second Triangle. This now completes the analogy between the two sets of shapes.

1. Level One

In a **Level One** analogy question, there is only one layer or change to look for within the first pair of shapes. This layer or change will then be applied to the second pair of shapes.

Example: Which shape completes the analogy?

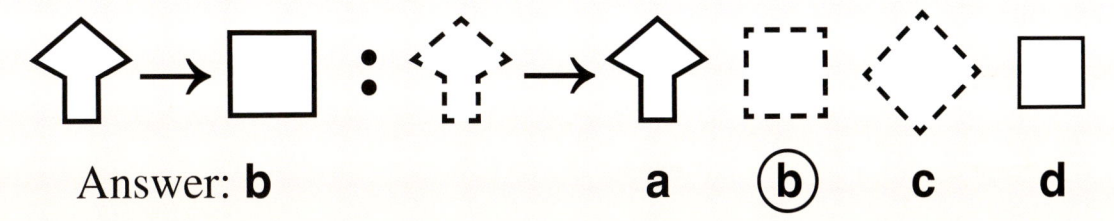

Answer: **b**   a   ⓑ   c   d

The Analogy Rule: In the first pair of shapes the Arrow Shape with a Solid Line becomes a Square with a Solid Line.
The Analogy Rule Applied: In the second pair of shapes the Arrow Shape with a Dashed Line becomes a Square with a Dashed Line.

Exercise 9: 1 Which shape or figure completes the analogy?

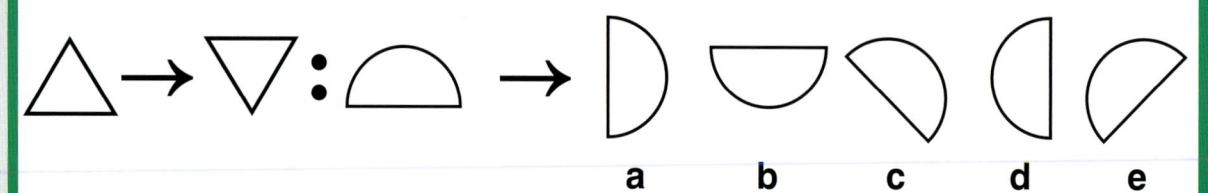

1) Analogy Rule: The shape rotates 180°. _____ Answer ____

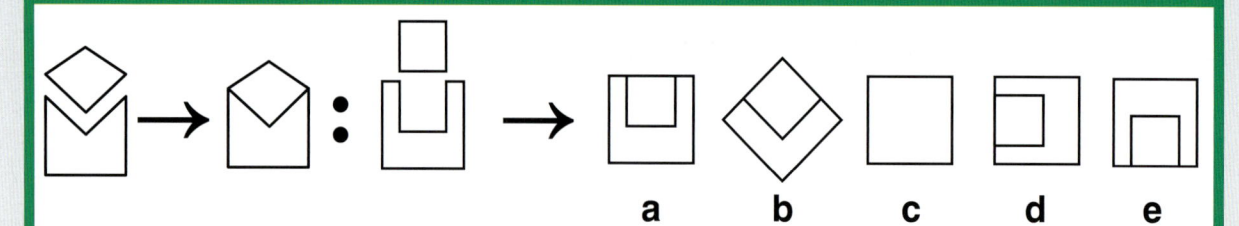

2) Analogy Rule: _____ Answer ____

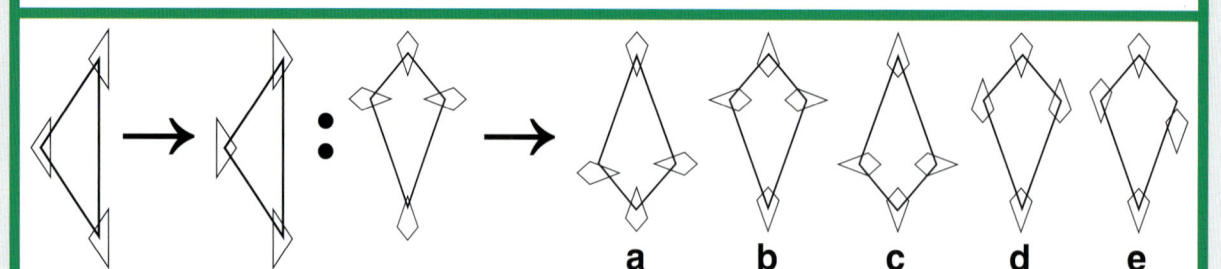

3) Analogy Rule: _____ Answer ____

4) Analogy Rule: _____ Answer ____

5) Analogy Rule: _____ Answer ____

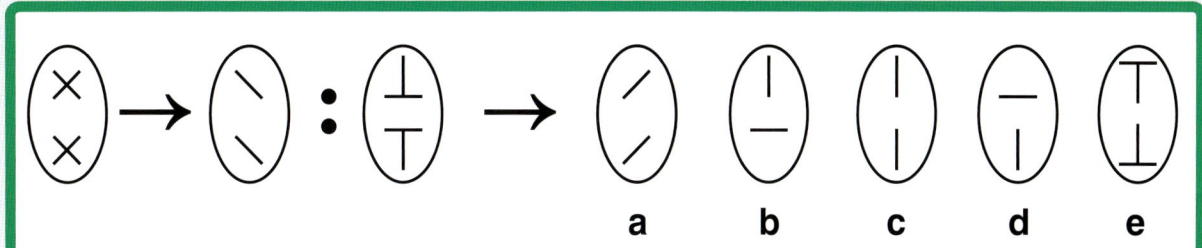

6) Analogy Rule: _____ Answer ____

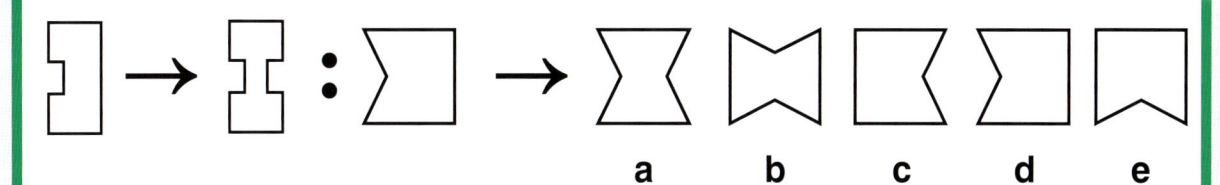

7) Analogy Rule: _____ Answer ____

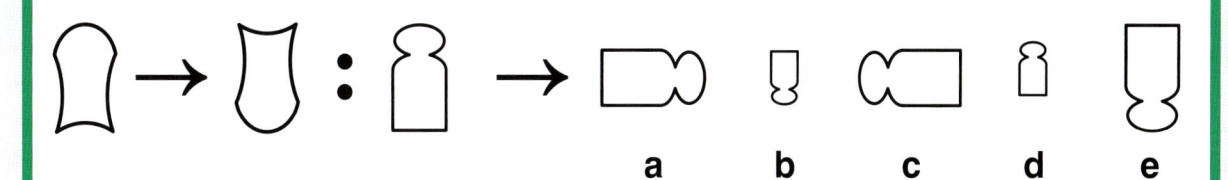

8) Analogy Rule: _____ Answer ____

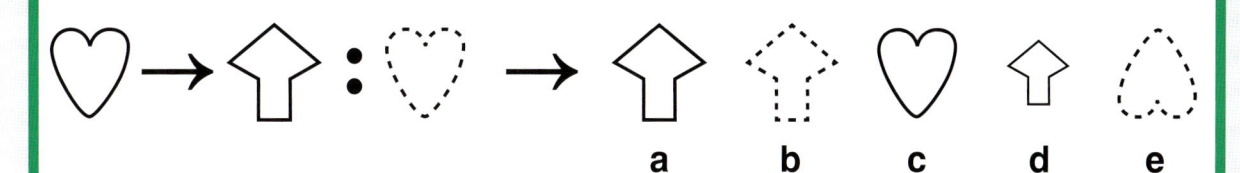

9) Analogy Rule: _____ Answer ____

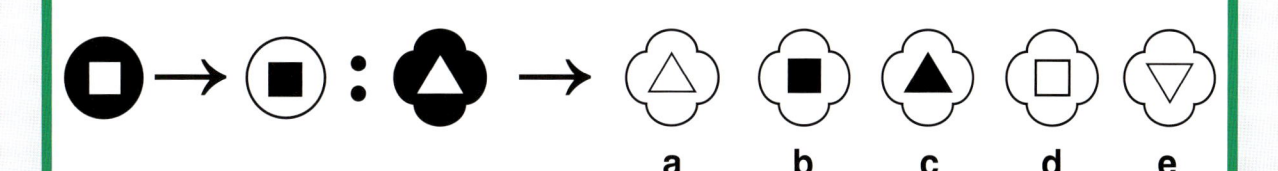

10) Analogy Rule: _____ Answer ____

Score ____

2. Level Two

In **Level Two** analogy questions, there are two layers or changes to look for in the first pair of figures. These layers or changes will then be applied to the second pair of figures.

Example: Which figure completes the analogy?

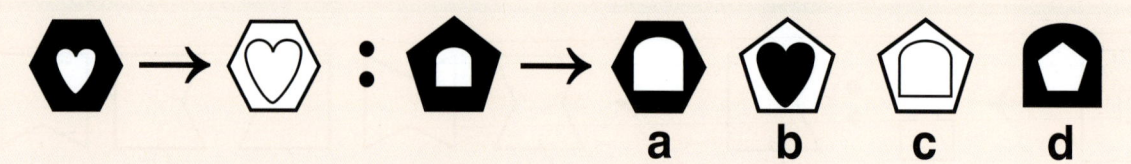

The First Pair of Figures - Analogy Rules:
In the first pair of figures there are two layers or changes:

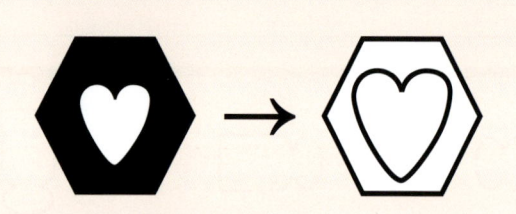

Layer 1 - The Regular Hexagon with a Black Fill becomes a Regular Hexagon with a White Fill. There is no change in size.

Layer 2 - The Heart Shape with a White Fill enlarges.

The Second Set of Figures:

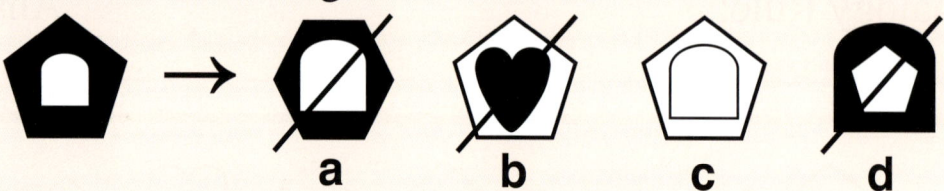

It is important to **eliminate** the wrong possibilities:

a - The Hexagon with a Black Fill should be a Pentagon with a White Fill.

b - The enclosed Heart Shape with a Black Fill should be an enclosed Loaf Shape with a White Fill.

d - The Loaf Shape with a Black Fill should be a Pentagon with a White Fill. The enclosed Pentagon with a White Fill should be an enclosed Loaf Shape with a White Fill.

The Correct Pair of Figures:
In this pairing we can identify the two correct layers or changes:

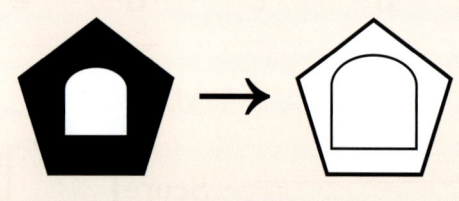

Layer 1 - The Regular Pentagon with a Black Fill becomes a Regular Pentagon with a White Fill.

Layer 2 - The Loaf Shape with a White Fill enlarges.

Answer: **c**

Exercise 9: 2   Which figure completes the analogy?

1) Analogy Rules:
i) The shape is rotated 90° anticlockwise.
ii) The same shape with the fills reversed is added.

Answer ____

2) Analogy Rules:
i) ____
ii) ____

Answer ____

3) Analogy Rules:
i) ____
ii) ____

Answer ____

4) Analogy Rules:
i) ____
ii) ____

Answer ____

5) Analogy Rules:
i) ____
ii) ____

Answer ____

© 2006 Stephen Curran

6) Analogy Rules:
   i) _____ Answer
   ii) _____ _____

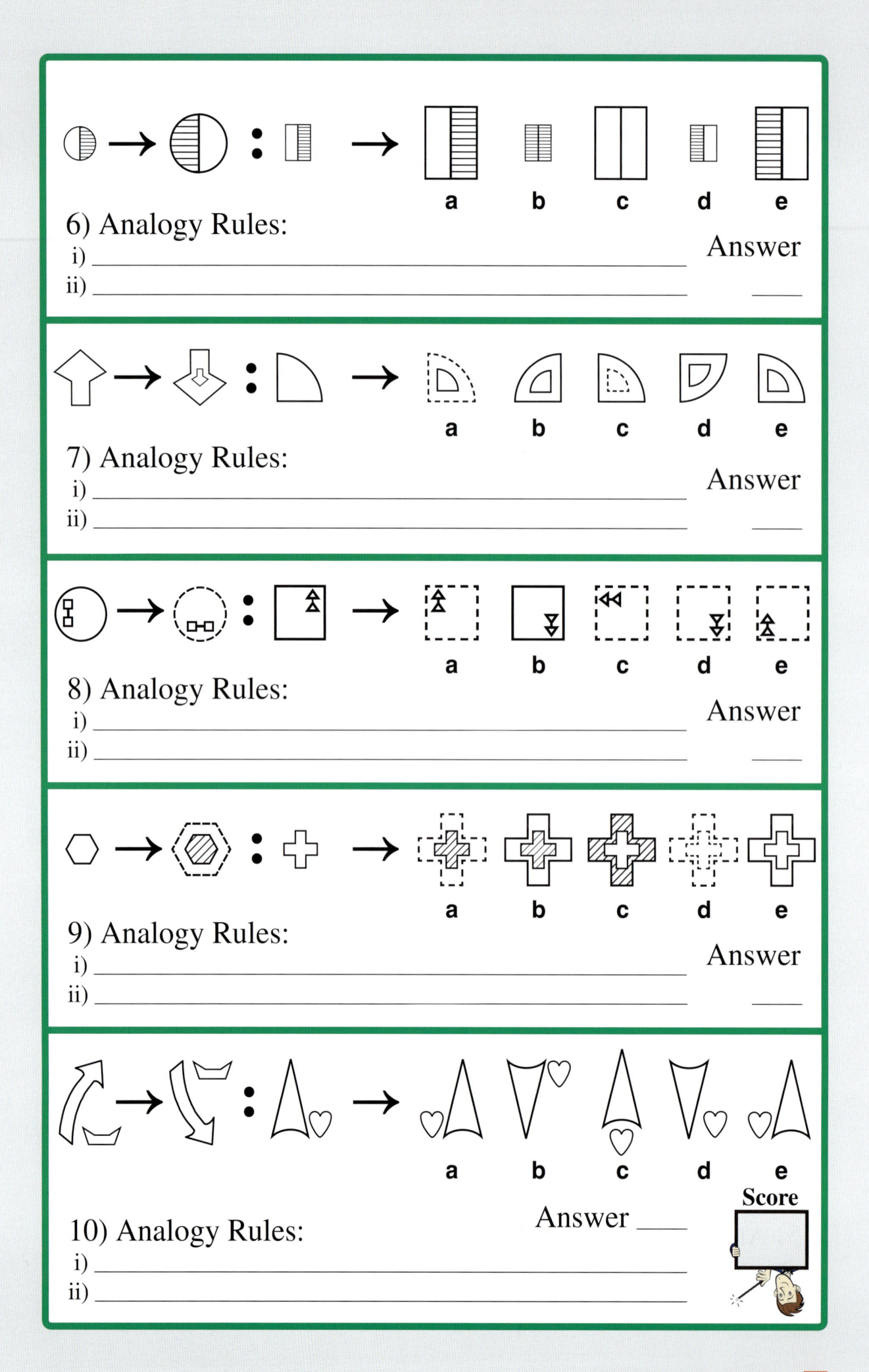

7) Analogy Rules:
   i) _____ Answer
   ii) _____ _____

8) Analogy Rules:
   i) _____ Answer
   ii) _____ _____

9) Analogy Rules:
   i) _____ Answer
   ii) _____ _____

10) Analogy Rules: Answer _____
    i) _____
    ii) _____

Score

3. Level Three

In **Level Three** analogy questions, there are three layers or changes to look for in the first pair of figures. These layers or changes will then be applied to the second pair of figures.

Example: Which figure completes the analogy?

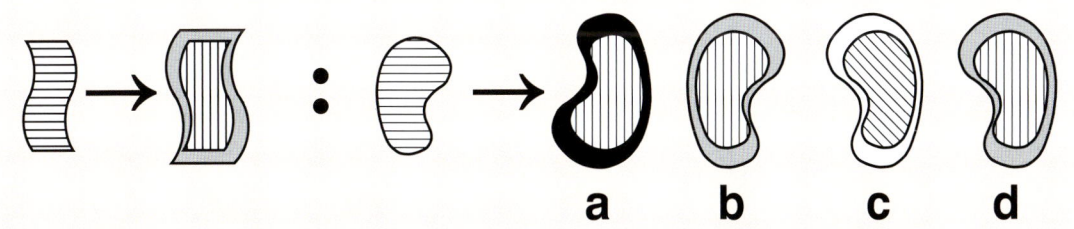

The First Pair of Figures - Analogy Rules:

In the first pair of figures there are three layers or changes:

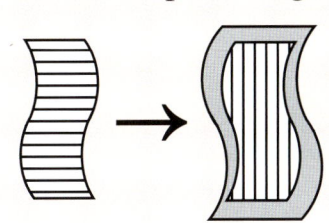

Layer 1 - The Ribbon Shape is reflected.
Layer 2 - The Horizontal Shaded Fill becomes a Vertical Shaded Fill.
Layer 3 - The Ribbon Shape is enclosed by a Larger Ribbon Shape with a Grey Fill.

The Second Set of Figures:

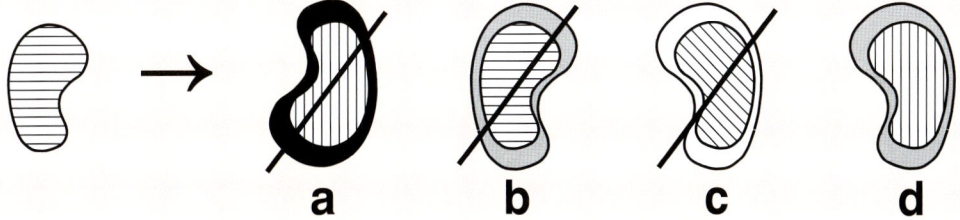

It is important to **eliminate** the wrong possibilities:

a - The enclosed Bean Shape has been rotated 180° and the outer Bean Shape has a Black Fill.

b - The enclosed Bean Shape has not been reflected and has a Horizontal Shaded Fill.

c - The enclosed Bean Shape has a Left Slanted Shaded Fill. The outer shape has a White Fill.

The Correct Pair of Figures:

In this pairing we can identify three correct layers or changes:

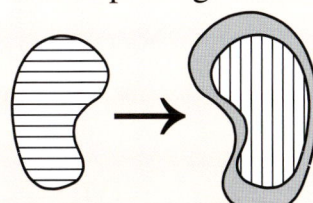

Layer 1 - The Bean Shape is reflected.
Layer 2 - The Horizontal Shaded Fill becomes a Vertical Shaded Fill.
Layer 3 - The smaller Bean Shape is enclosed by a larger Bean Shape with a Grey Fill.

Answer: **d**

© 2006 Stephen Curran

Exercise 9: 3
Which figure completes the analogy?

1) Analogy Rules:
   i) The figure reduces.
   ii) The figure rotates 45° anticlockwise.
   iii) The same shape with a Black Fill is added above the first shape.

   Answer ____

2) Analogy Rules:
   i) ____
   ii) ____
   iii) ____

   Answer ____

3) Analogy Rules:
   i) ____
   ii) ____
   iii) ____

   Answer ____

4) Analogy Rules:
   i) ____
   ii) ____
   iii) ____

   Answer ____

5) Analogy Rules:
   i) ____
   ii) ____
   iii) ____

   Answer ____

6) Analogy Rules:
   i) _____
   ii) _____ Answer
   iii) _____ ____

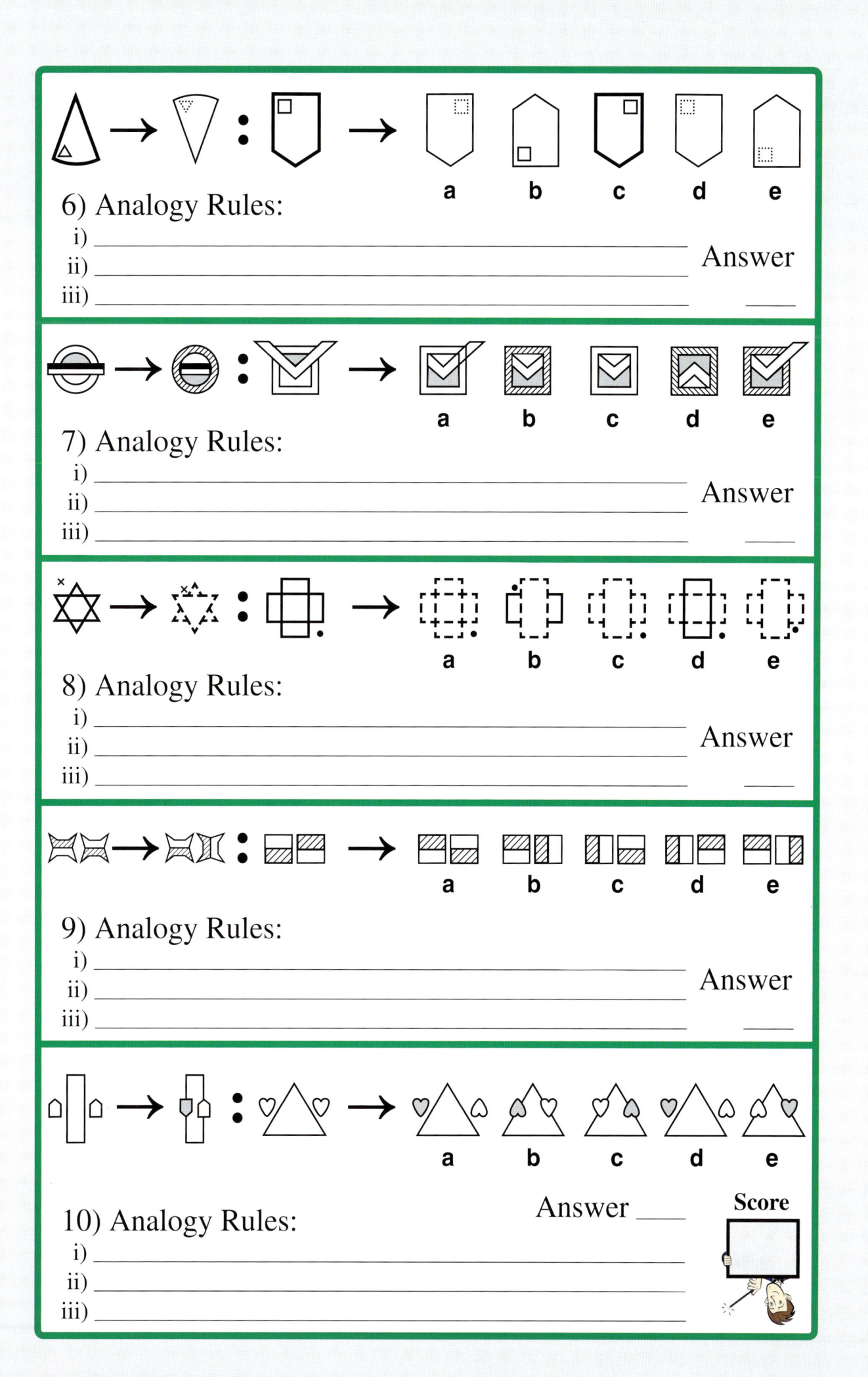

7) Analogy Rules:
   i) _____
   ii) _____ Answer
   iii) _____ ____

8) Analogy Rules:
   i) _____
   ii) _____ Answer
   iii) _____ ____

9) Analogy Rules:
   i) _____
   ii) _____ Answer
   iii) _____ ____

10) Analogy Rules:
    i) _____
    ii) _____ Answer ____
    iii) _____

Score

© 2006 Stephen Curran

4. Levels Four & Five

In **Level Four** or **Five** analogy questions, there are four or five layers or changes to look for in the first pair of figures. These layers or changes are then applied to the second pair of figures.

Example: Which figure completes the analogy?

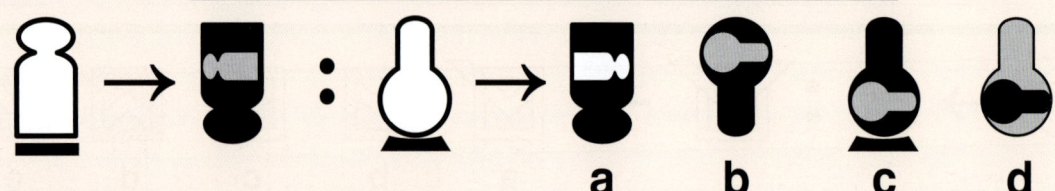

a b c d

The First Pair of Figures:

In the first pair of figures there are four layers or changes:

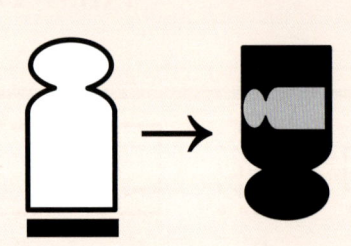

Layer 1 - The Churn Shape has been rotated 180°.
Layer 2 - The White Fill has become a Black Fill.
Layer 3 - A reduced Churn Shape with a Grey Fill, rotated at 90°, has been enclosed within the second Churn Shape.
Layer 4 - The Rectangle with a Black Fill has been subtracted.

The Second Set of Figures:

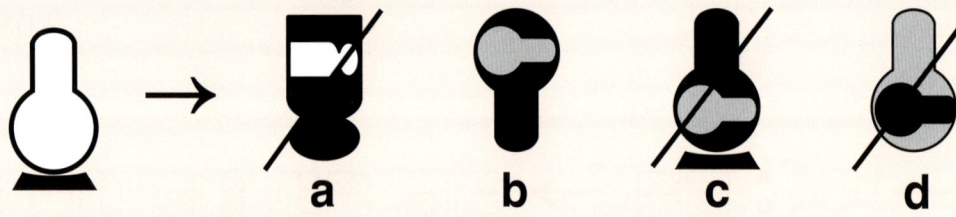

a b c d

It is important to **eliminate** the wrong possibilities:

a - The Churn Shape is the wrong shape and the enclosed shape should have a Grey Fill.
c - The Bulb Shape has not been rotated and the Blade Shape has not been subtracted.
d - The outer Bulb Shape has not been rotated, has a Grey Fill and the enclosed Bulb Shape has a Black Fill.

The Correct Pair of Figures:

In this pairing we can identify four correct layers or changes:

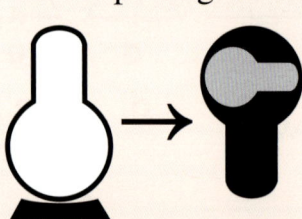

Layer 1 - The Bulb Shape has been rotated 180°.
Layer 2 - The White Fill has become a Black Fill.
Layer 3 - A reduced Bulb Shape with a Grey Fill, rotated at 90°, has been enclosed within the second Bulb Shape.
Layer 4 - The Blade Shape with a Black Fill has been subtracted.

Answer: **b**

Exercise 9: 4   Which figure completes the analogy?

1) **Analogy Rules:**
   i) The figure rotates 90° Anticlockwise.
   ii) A Dashed Line is added across the middle of the figure.
   iii) The two enclosed shapes swap places (transpose).
   iv) An Ellipse with a Grey Fill is added to the outside of the figure.

   Answer ____

2) **Analogy Rules:**
   i) _____
   ii) _____
   iii) _____
   iv) _____

   Answer ____

3) **Analogy Rules:**
   i) _____
   ii) _____
   iii) _____
   iv) _____

   Answer ____

4) **Analogy Rules:**
   i) _____
   ii) _____
   iii) _____
   iv) _____

   Answer ____

5) **Analogy Rules:**
   i) _____
   ii) _____
   iii) _____
   iv) _____

   Answer ____

© 2006 Stephen Curran

6) Analogy Rules:
   i) _____
   ii) _____
   iii) _____ Answer
   iv) _____ _____

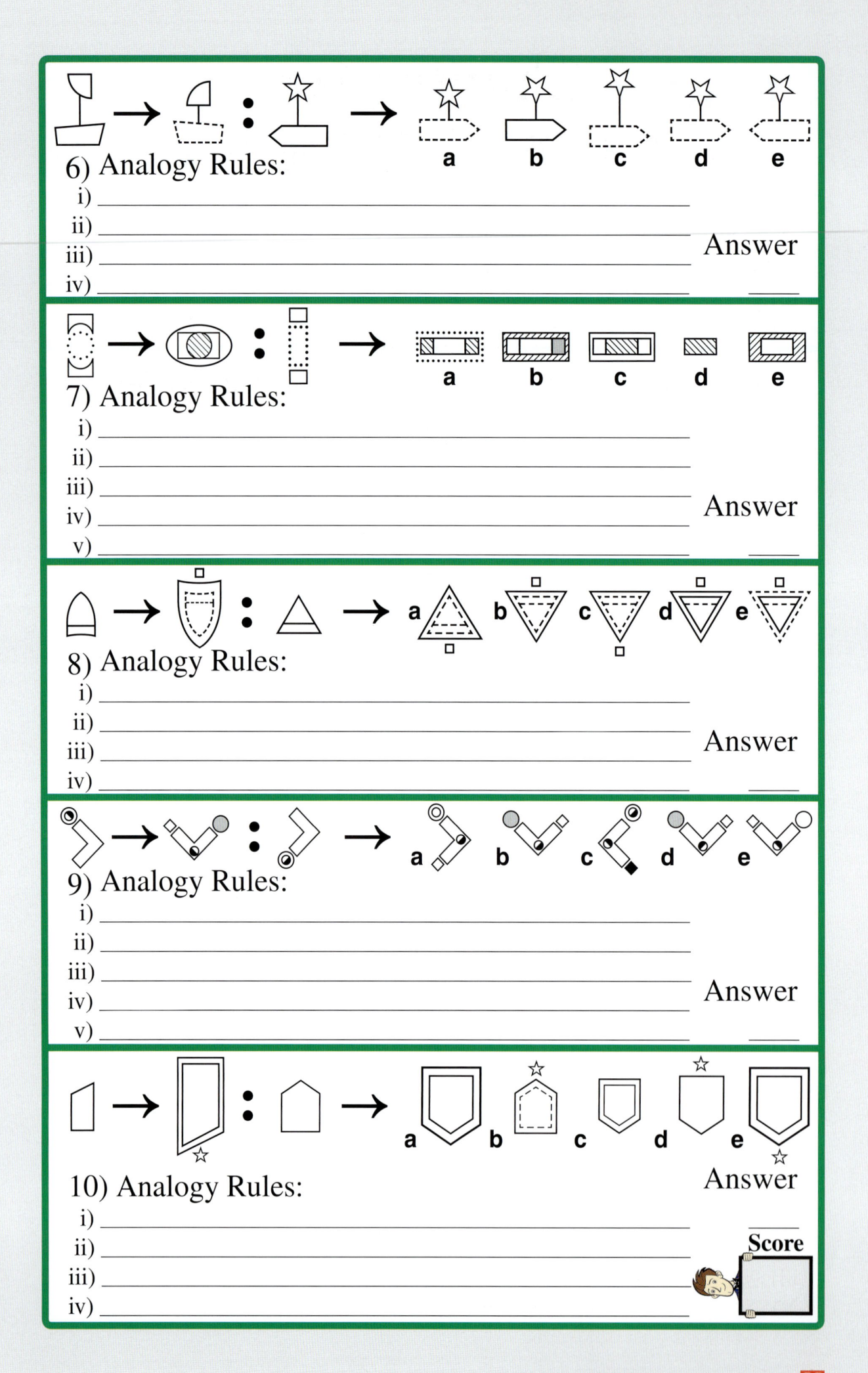

7) Analogy Rules:
   i) _____
   ii) _____
   iii) _____
   iv) _____ Answer
   v) _____ _____

8) Analogy Rules:
   i) _____
   ii) _____
   iii) _____ Answer
   iv) _____ _____

9) Analogy Rules:
   i) _____
   ii) _____
   iii) _____
   iv) _____ Answer
   v) _____ _____

10) Analogy Rules:
   i) _____
   ii) _____
   iii) _____ Score
   iv) _____

Chapter Ten
SIMILARITIES

In Verbal Reasoning, **Similarity** questions involve selecting two words from two groups that have the closest meaning.

For example: (**conclude   transmit   start**)
(**organise   begin   associate**)

The two words most similar in meaning are **start** and **begin**. In a Non-verbal Reasoning similarity question, a strong likeness can be established between two or more shapes.

Example:

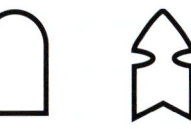

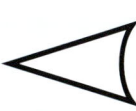

The two Shield Shapes are most similar as they belong to the same family of shapes.

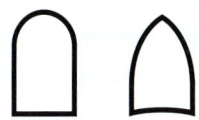

1. Level One

In **Level One** similarity questions, there is only one layer or similarity to look for between the shapes or figures.

Example: Which figure on the right is most like the two figures on the left?

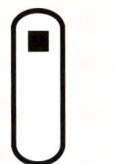

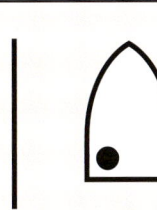

a   b   c   ⓓ   e

Answer: **d**

The Similarity Rule that connects the figures on the left is: A small Square with a Black Fill must be enclosed within the larger shape. This is only true for figure **d**.

Note: A similarity rule only counts if it helps select the correct alternative by eliminating the wrong ones. In the above example, all the figures have an enclosed shape with a Black Fill. As they all share this similarity, it does not count as a similarity rule.

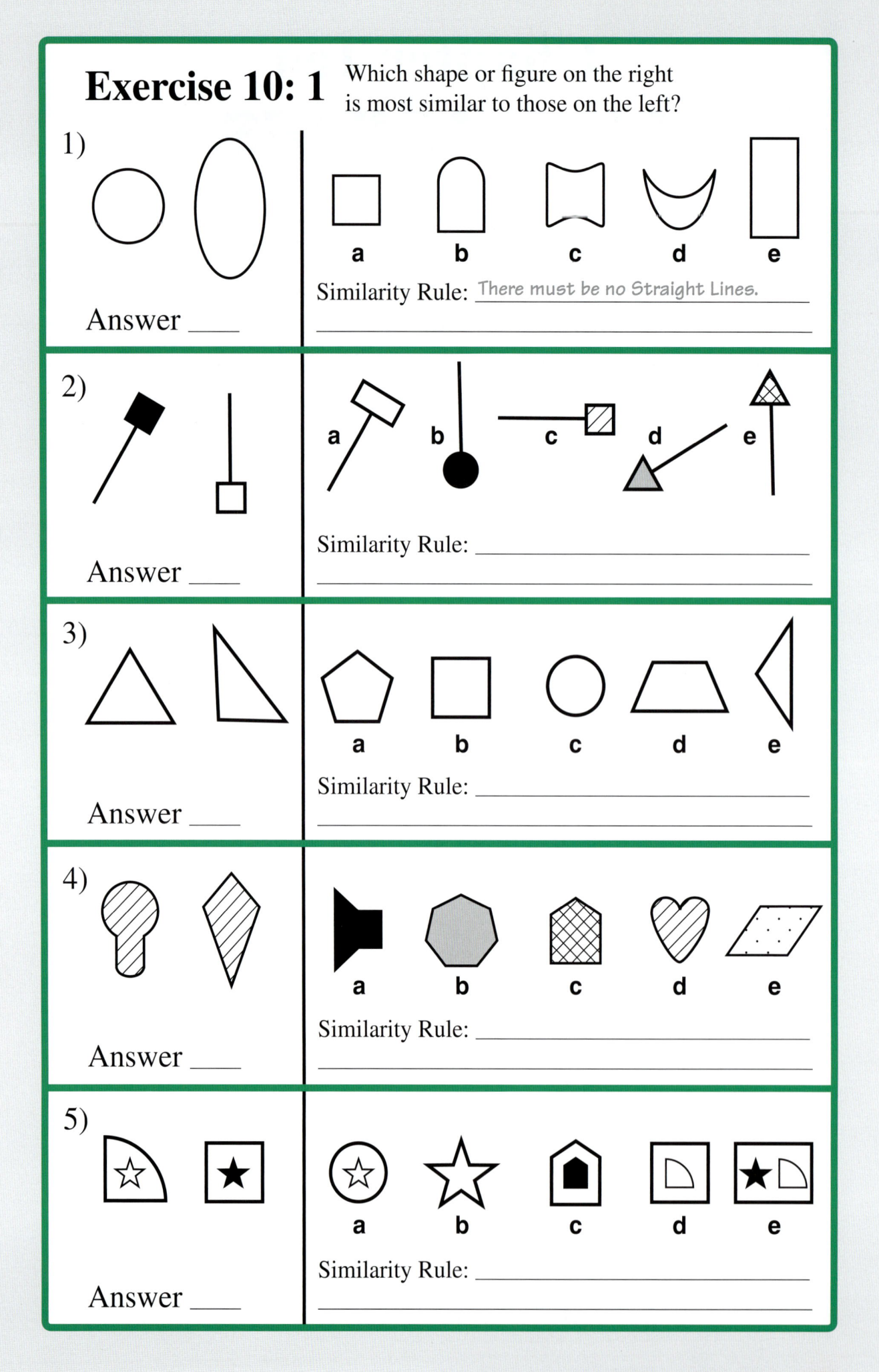

Exercise 10: 1

Which shape or figure on the right is most similar to those on the left?

1) Answer ____
Similarity Rule: There must be no Straight Lines.

2) Answer ____
Similarity Rule: ____

3) Answer ____
Similarity Rule: ____

4) Answer ____
Similarity Rule: ____

5) Answer ____
Similarity Rule: ____

6) Answer ____

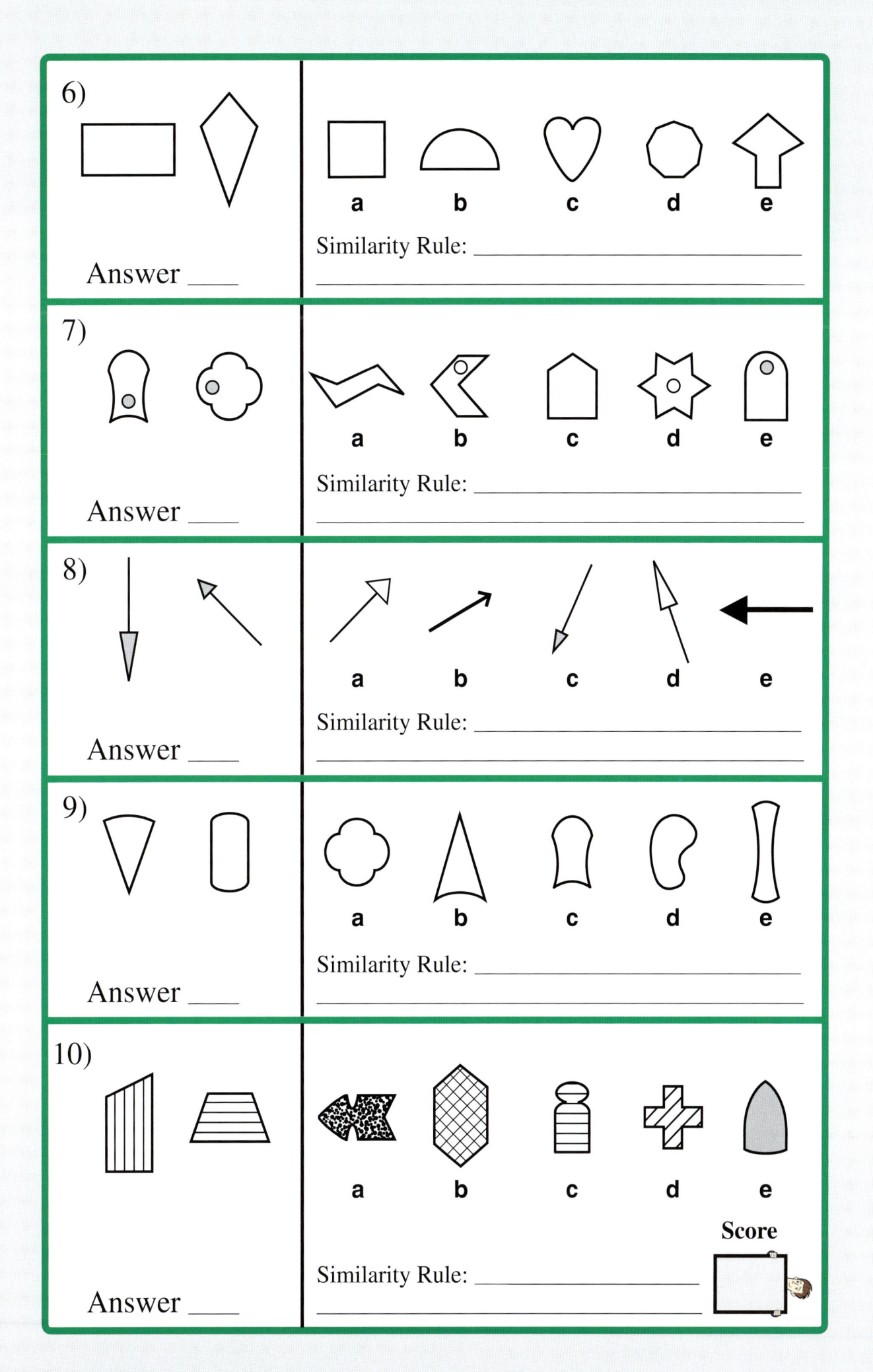

a b c d e

Similarity Rule: _____

7) Answer ____

a b c d e

Similarity Rule: _____

8) Answer ____

a b c d e

Similarity Rule: _____

9) Answer ____

a b c d e

Similarity Rule: _____

10) Answer ____

a b c d e

Similarity Rule: _____

Score

© 2006 Stephen Curran

2. Level Two

In **Level Two** similarity questions, there are two layers or similarities to look for between the figures.

Example: Which figure on the right is most like the two figures on the left?

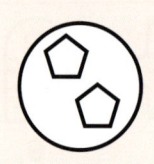

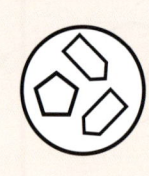

a   b   c   d

The Rules of Similarity:

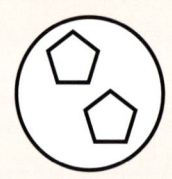

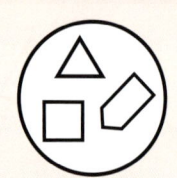

Layer 1 - The shapes are either identical or completely different.
Layer 2 - The shapes are either in groups of two or three.

Remember: The rules are only relevant if they help to select the right alternative and eliminate the wrong ones.

The Set of Figures:

a   b   c   d

It is important to **eliminate** the wrong possibilities:
a - There are two identical shapes and one shape is different.
b - There should be no more than three shapes.
c - There are two identical shapes and one shape is different.

The Correct Figure:

This figure follows the rules of similarity.
Layer 1 - All the Triangles are identical.
Layer 2 - The Triangles are in a group of three.

Answer: **d**

Exercise 10: 2 — Which figure on the right is most similar to those on the left?

1)

    a   b   c   d   e

Similarity Rules → i) The shapes must be different sizes.
Answer ____ ii) The fills: two largest shapes - Black; smallest - White.

2)

    a   b   c   d   e

Similarity Rules → i) ____
Answer ____ ii) ____

3)

    a   b   c   d   e

Similarity Rules → i) ____
Answer ____ ii) ____

4)

    a   b   c   d   e

Similarity Rules → i) ____
Answer ____ ii) ____

5)

    a   b   c   d   e

Similarity Rules → i) ____
Answer ____ ii) ____

© 2006 Stephen Curran

6)

Similarity Rules → i) _____
Answer ____   ii) _____

7)

Similarity Rules → i) _____
Answer ____   ii) _____

8)

Similarity Rules → i) _____
Answer ____   ii) _____

9)

Similarity Rules → i) _____
Answer ____   ii) _____

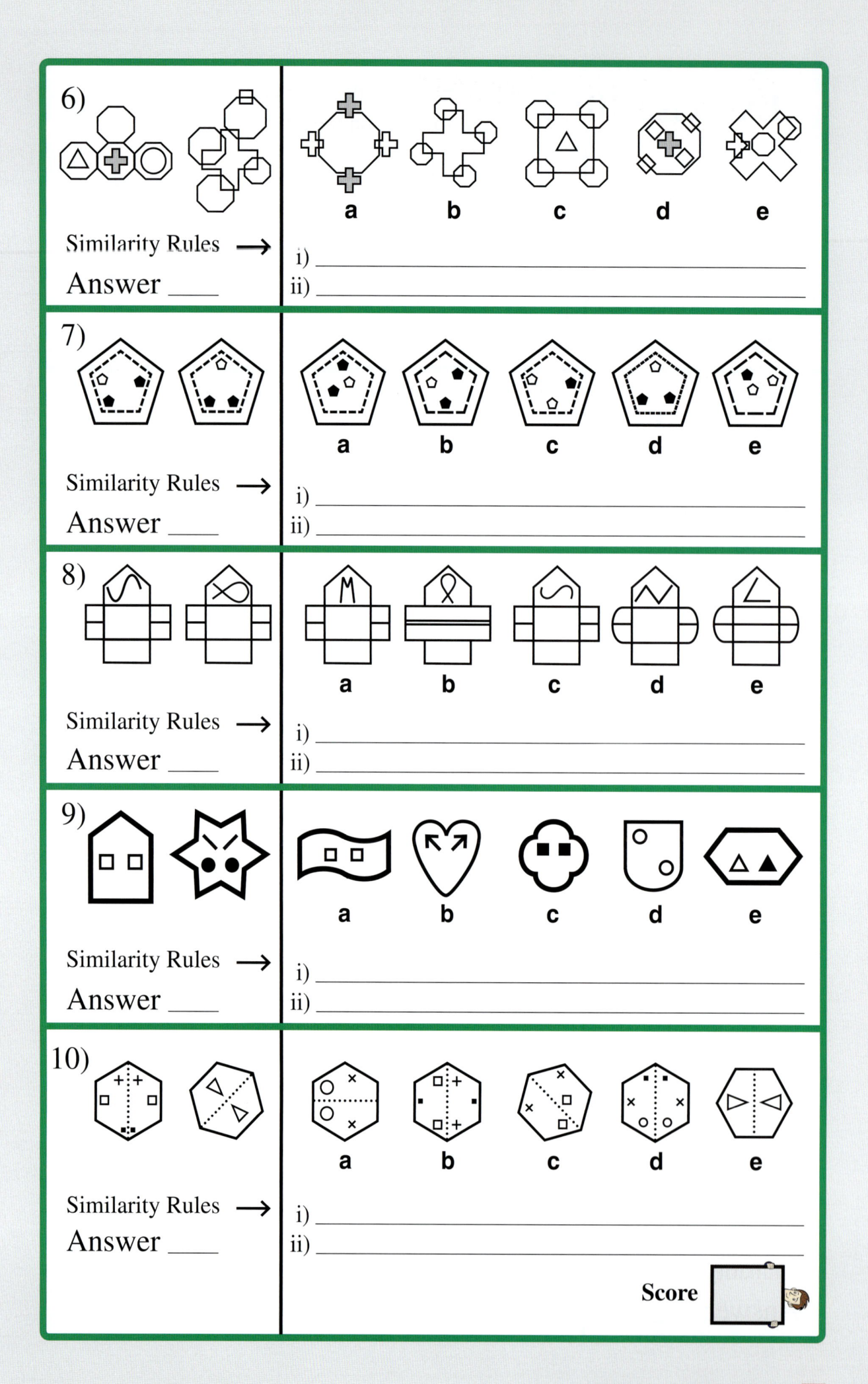

10)

Similarity Rules → i) _____
Answer ____   ii) _____

Score ____

3. Level Three

In **Level Three** similarity questions, there are three layers or similarities to look for between the figures.

Example: Which figure on the right is most like the two figures on the left?

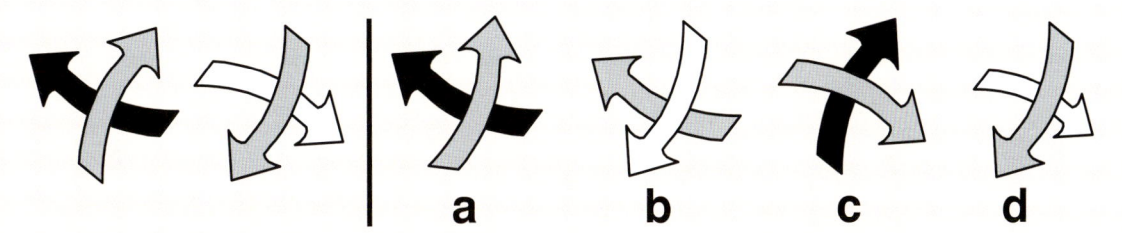

a   b   c   d

The Rules of Similarity:

Layer 1 - The Arrow Shapes are the same size.
Layer 2 - The Arrow Shape with a Grey Fill always overlays the second Arrow Shape.
Layer 3 - The two Arrow Shapes are related by rotation (a rotational difference of 90°).

Remember: The rules are only relevant if they help to select the right alternative and eliminate the wrong ones.

The Set of Figures:

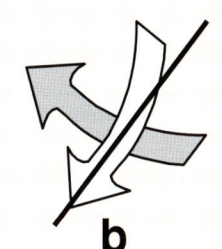

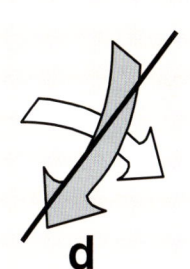

a   b   c   d

It is important to **eliminate** the wrong possibilities:
a - The Arrow Shapes are not rotations but inversions of each other.
b - The Arrow Shape with a White Fill forms the overlay.
d - The Arrow Shape with a White Fill is smaller than the other Arrow Shape.

The Correct Figure:

This figure follows the rules of similarity.
Layer 1 - Both Arrow Shapes are the same size.
Layer 2 - The Arrow Shape with a Grey Fill overlays the second Arrow Shape with a Black Fill.
Layer 3 - The two Arrow Shapes are related by rotation (a rotational difference of 90°).

Answer: **c**

© 2006 Stephen Curran

Exercise 10: 3

Which figure on the right is most similar to those on the left?

1)

Similarity Rules →
Answer ___

i) The shape is in two halves: Shaded and White Fill.
ii) The shading is perpendicular to the centre line.
iii) The shape must rest on a horizontal base.

2)

Similarity Rules →
Answer ___

i) _____
ii) _____
iii) _____

3)

Similarity Rules →
Answer ___

i) _____
ii) _____
iii) _____

4)

Similarity Rules →
Answer ___

i) _____
ii) _____
iii) _____

5)

Similarity Rules →
Answer ___

i) _____
ii) _____
iii) _____

42 © 2006 Stephen Curran

6)

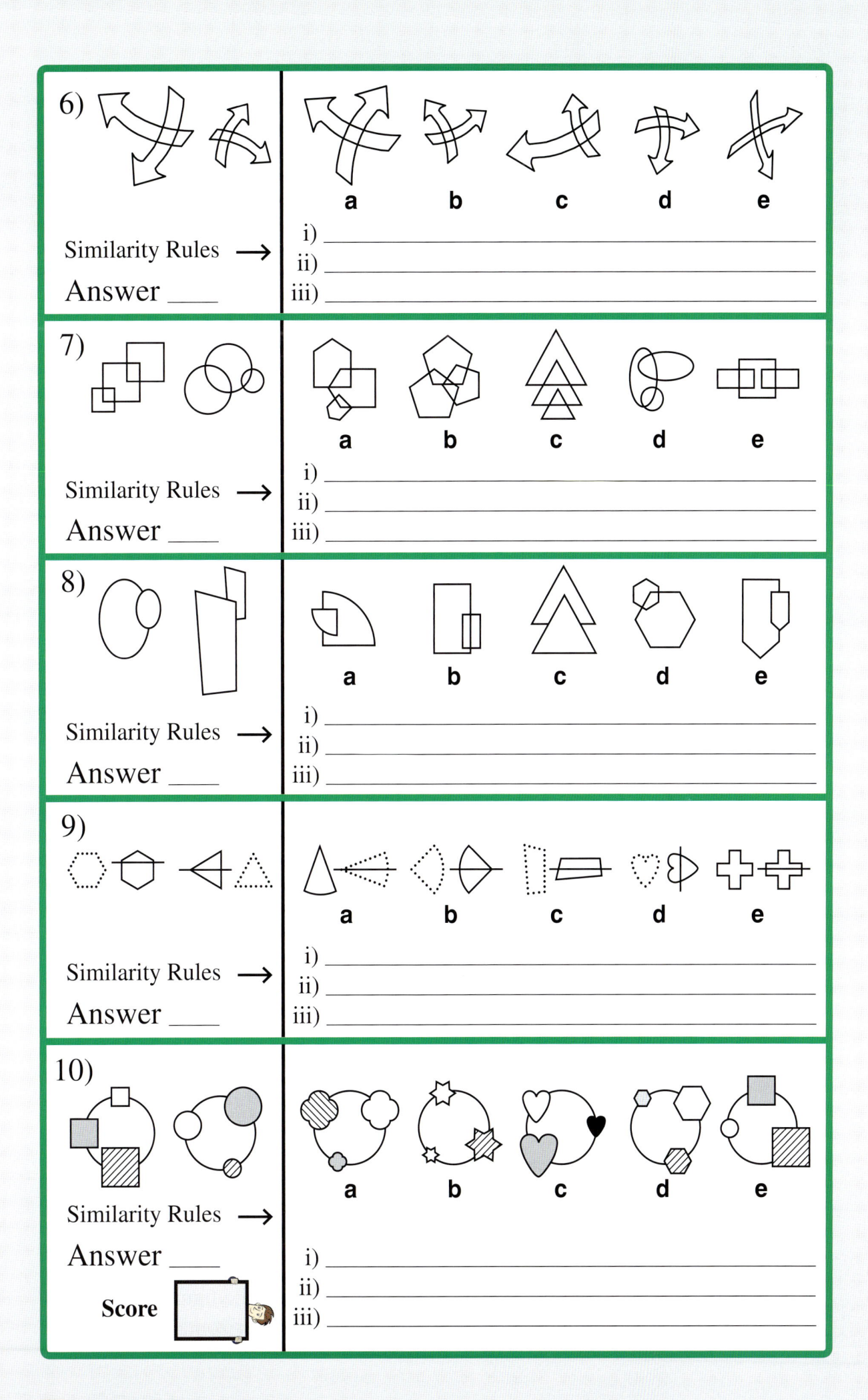

Similarity Rules →

Answer ____

a   b   c   d   e

i) ____
ii) ____
iii) ____

7)

Similarity Rules →

Answer ____

a   b   c   d   e

i) ____
ii) ____
iii) ____

8)

Similarity Rules →

Answer ____

a   b   c   d   e

i) ____
ii) ____
iii) ____

9)

Similarity Rules →

Answer ____

a   b   c   d   e

i) ____
ii) ____
iii) ____

10)

Similarity Rules →

Answer ____

Score ____

a   b   c   d   e

i) ____
ii) ____
iii) ____

© 2006 Stephen Curran

43

4. Levels Four & Five

In **Level Four** or **Five** similarity questions, there are four or five layers or similarities to look for between the figures.

Example: Which figure on the right is most like the two figures on the left?

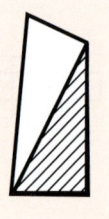

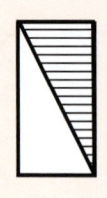

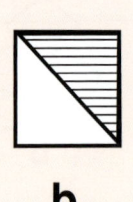

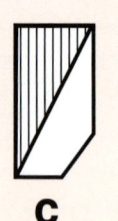

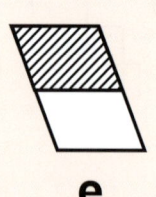

a   b   c   d   e

The Rules of Similarity:

Layer 1 - The figures are always Quadrilaterals.
Layer 2 - A diagonal line always divides the figures.
Layer 3 - The direction of the shaded fills never follows the diagonal line that divides the figures.
Layer 4 - The base of the figure must be horizontal.

Remember: The rules are only relevant if they help to select the right alternative and eliminate the wrong ones.

The Set of Figures:

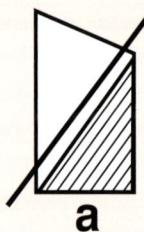

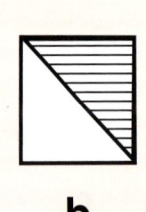

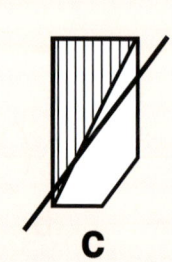

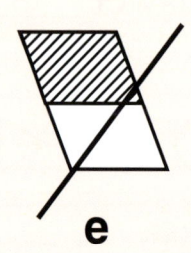

a   b   c   d   e

It is important to **eliminate** the wrong possibilities:

a - The shading follows the direction of the diagonal.
c - The figure is not a Quadrilateral Shape.
d - The figure does not have a horizontal base.
e - The figure has a horizontal line rather than a diagonal line.

The Correct Figure:

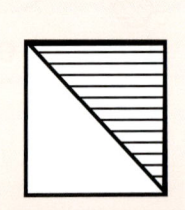

This figure follows the rules of similarity.
Layer 1 - The figure is a Quadrilateral.
Layer 2 - A diagonal line divides the figure.
Layer 3 - The direction of the shaded fill does not follow the diagonal line that divides the figure.
Layer 4 - The base of the figure is horizontal.

Answer: **b**

Exercise 10: 4

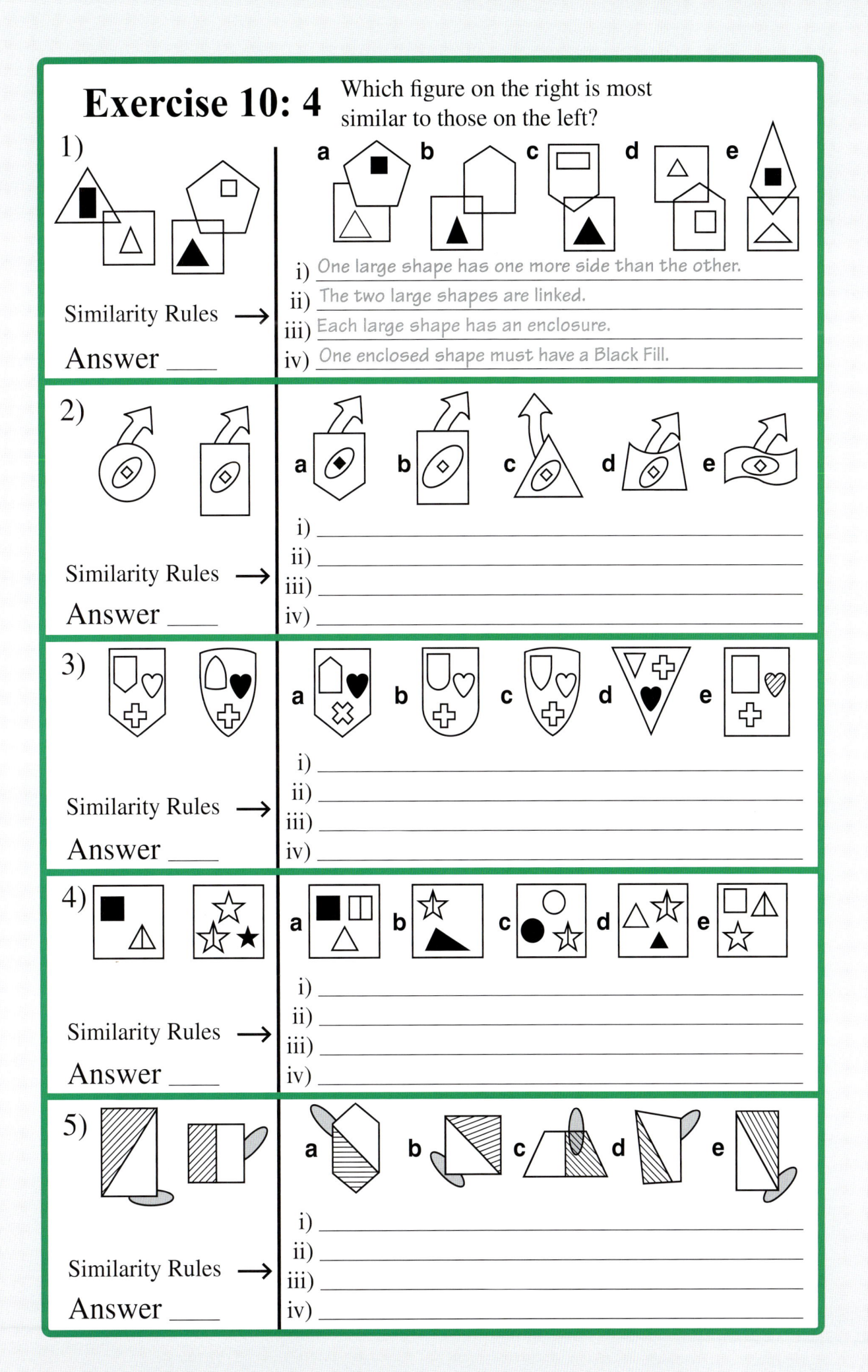

Which figure on the right is most similar to those on the left?

1)

Similarity Rules →
Answer ____

i) One large shape has one more side than the other.
ii) The two large shapes are linked.
iii) Each large shape has an enclosure.
iv) One enclosed shape must have a Black Fill.

2)

Similarity Rules →
Answer ____

i) ____
ii) ____
iii) ____
iv) ____

3)

Similarity Rules →
Answer ____

i) ____
ii) ____
iii) ____
iv) ____

4)

Similarity Rules →
Answer ____

i) ____
ii) ____
iii) ____
iv) ____

5)

Similarity Rules →
Answer ____

i) ____
ii) ____
iii) ____
iv) ____

© 2006 Stephen Curran

6) Similarity Rules →
Answer ____
 i) _____
 ii) _____
 iii) _____
 iv) _____

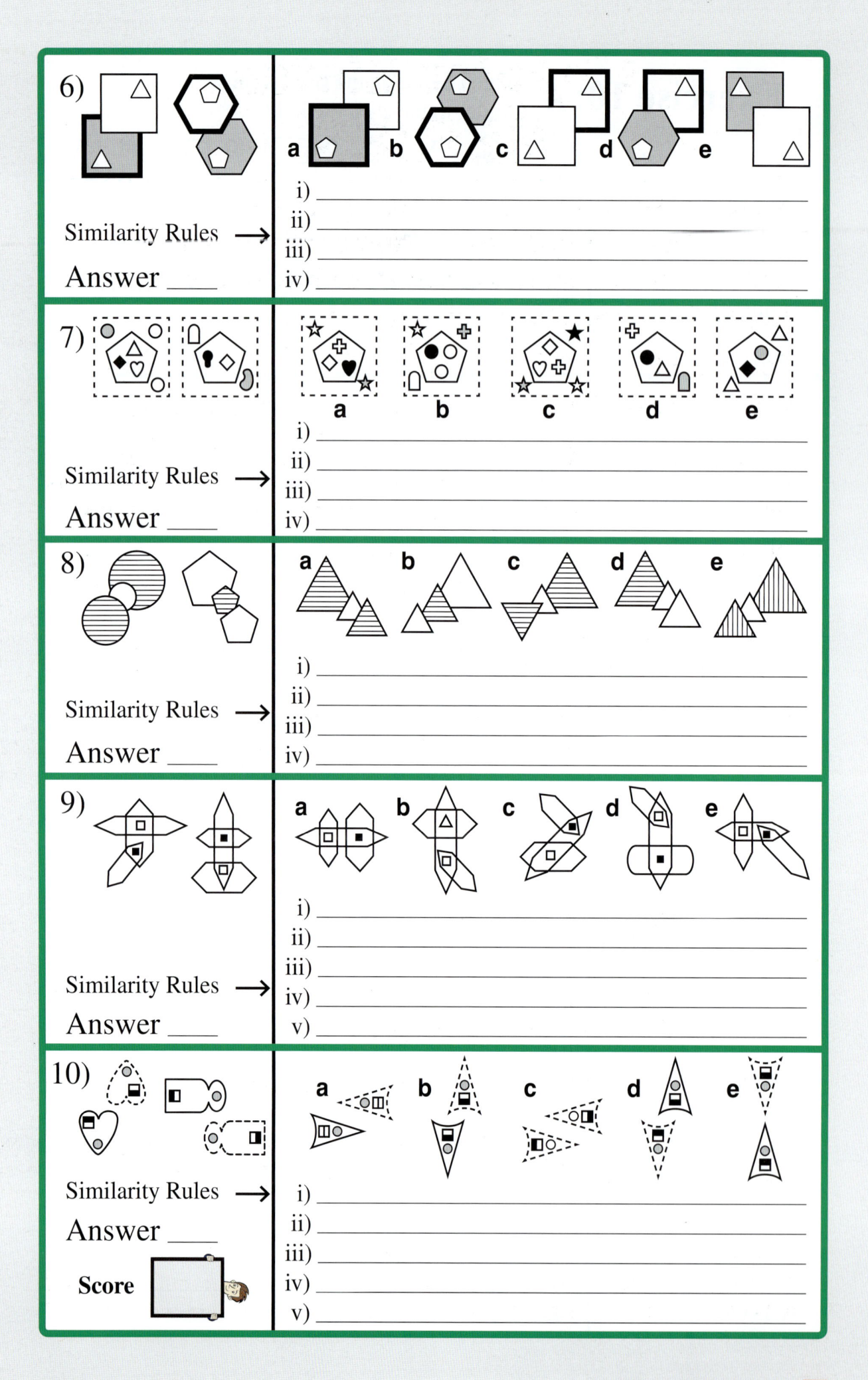

7) Similarity Rules →
Answer ____
 i) _____
 ii) _____
 iii) _____
 iv) _____

8) Similarity Rules →
Answer ____
 i) _____
 ii) _____
 iii) _____
 iv) _____

9) Similarity Rules →
Answer ____
 i) _____
 ii) _____
 iii) _____
 iv) _____
 v) _____

10) Similarity Rules →
Answer ____
Score
 i) _____
 ii) _____
 iii) _____
 iv) _____
 v) _____

Chapter Eleven
SERIES

Series questions in Verbal Reasoning can be either:
Letter Sequences or **Number Sequences**
Letter or number patterns can be **Repetitive** or **Cumulative**.
Repetitive - One letter is missing each time.

For example: A ᴮ C ᴰ E ᶠ G ᴴ I ᴶ K ᴸ M ᴺ O

Cumulative - The gap between the numbers gets larger.

For example: 1 ⁺² 3 ⁺³ 6 ⁺⁴ 10 ⁺⁵ 15 ⁺⁶ 21 ⁺⁷ 28

Series questions in Non-verbal Reasoning are of two types:
Shapes can be arranged in a repetitive pattern:

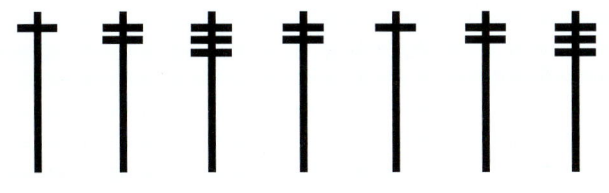

The Telegraph Poles are in a repetitive pattern of one, two, three, two, one, two, three crossbars, etc.

Shapes can be be arranged in a Cumulative Pattern:

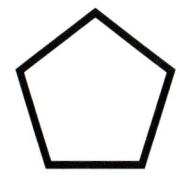

The Pentagon builds side by side in five stages.

1. Level One

In **Level One** series questions, there is only one layer or change to look for between the shapes or figures.

Example: Which shape is missing in the series?

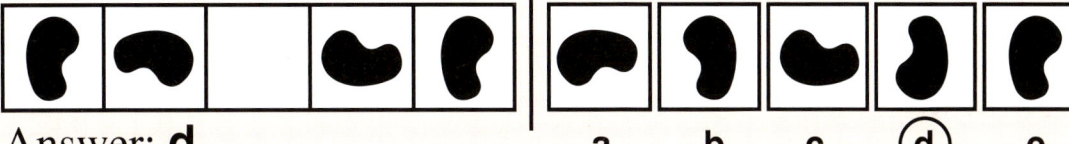

Answer: **d**   a   b   c   ⓓ   e
The Bean Shape is rotated 90° clockwise each time.
Note: In series questions, a rule only occurs if it indicates something that changes as the series progresses, e.g. we do not need to say the shape is always a Bean.

Exercise 11: 1

Which shape or figure on the right completes the series on the left?

1) Answer ____

a b c d e

Series Rule: The figure rotates 90° anticlockwise each stage.

Repetitive or Cumulative? Repetitive.

2) Answer ____

a b c d e

Series Rule: ____

Repetitive or Cumulative? ____

3) Answer ____

a b c d e

Series Rule: ____

Repetitive or Cumulative? ____

4) Answer ____

a b c d e

Series Rule: ____

Repetitive or Cumulative? ____

5) Answer ____

a b c d e

Series Rule: ____

Repetitive or Cumulative? ____

© 2006 Stephen Curran

6)

Series Rule: _____

Answer ____

a b c d e

Repetitive or Cumulative? _____

7)

Series Rule: _____

Answer ____

a b c d e

Repetitive or Cumulative? _____

8)

Series Rule: _____

Answer ____

a b c d e

Repetitive or Cumulative? _____

9)

Series Rule: _____

Answer ____

a b c d e

Repetitive or Cumulative? _____

10)

Series Rule: _____

Answer ____

a b c d e

Repetitive or Cumulative? _____

Score

2. Level Two

In **Level Two** series questions, there are two layers or changes to look for in the sequence of shapes or figures.

Example: Which figure is missing in the series?

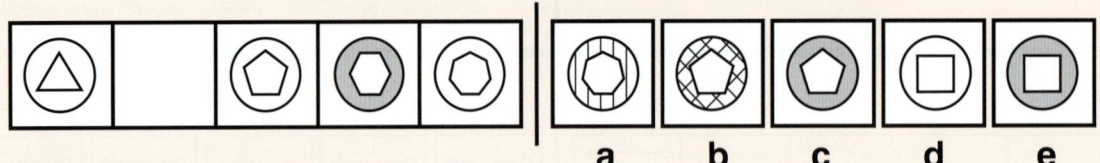

a b c d e

The Series Rules:

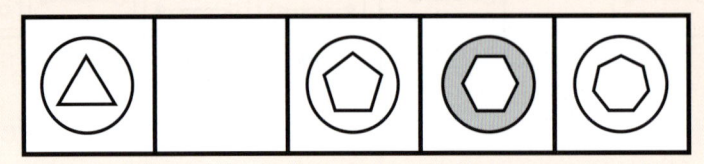

Layer 1 - The fills in the Circle alternate between White and Grey (repetitive).

Layer 2 - The frequency (number) of sides of the enclosed shape increases by one each stage (cumulative).

Remember: In series questions, a rule only occurs if it indicates something that changes as the series progresses, e.g. we do not need to say the outer shape is always a Circle.

The Set of Figures:

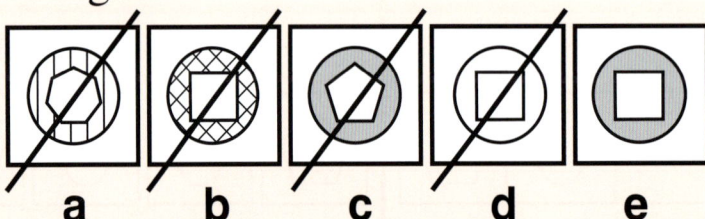

a b c d e

It is important to **eliminate** the wrong possibilities:

a - The Circle has a Shaded Fill and the enclosed shape is a Heptagon.
b - The Circle has a Cross-hatched Lattice Fill.
c - The enclosed shape is a Pentagon.
d - The Circle has a White Fill.

The Correct Figure:

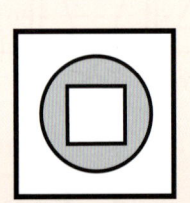

This figure follows the series rules.

Layer 1 - The fill in the Circle should be Grey (repetitive).

Layer 2 - The enclosed shape should have four sides (cumulative).

Answer: **e**

Exercise 11: 2

Which figure on the right completes the series on the left?

1)

Answer ____

Series Rules:
i) The Square with a Grey Fill rotates clockwise around the figure.
ii) A quarter of the Circle is added at each stage in an anticlockwise direction.

2)

Answer ____

Series Rules:
i) ____
ii) ____

3)

Answer ____

Series Rules:
i) ____
ii) ____

4)

Answer ____

Series Rules:
i) ____
ii) ____

5)

Answer ____

Series Rules:
i) ____
ii) ____

© 2006 Stephen Curran

51

6) Answer ____

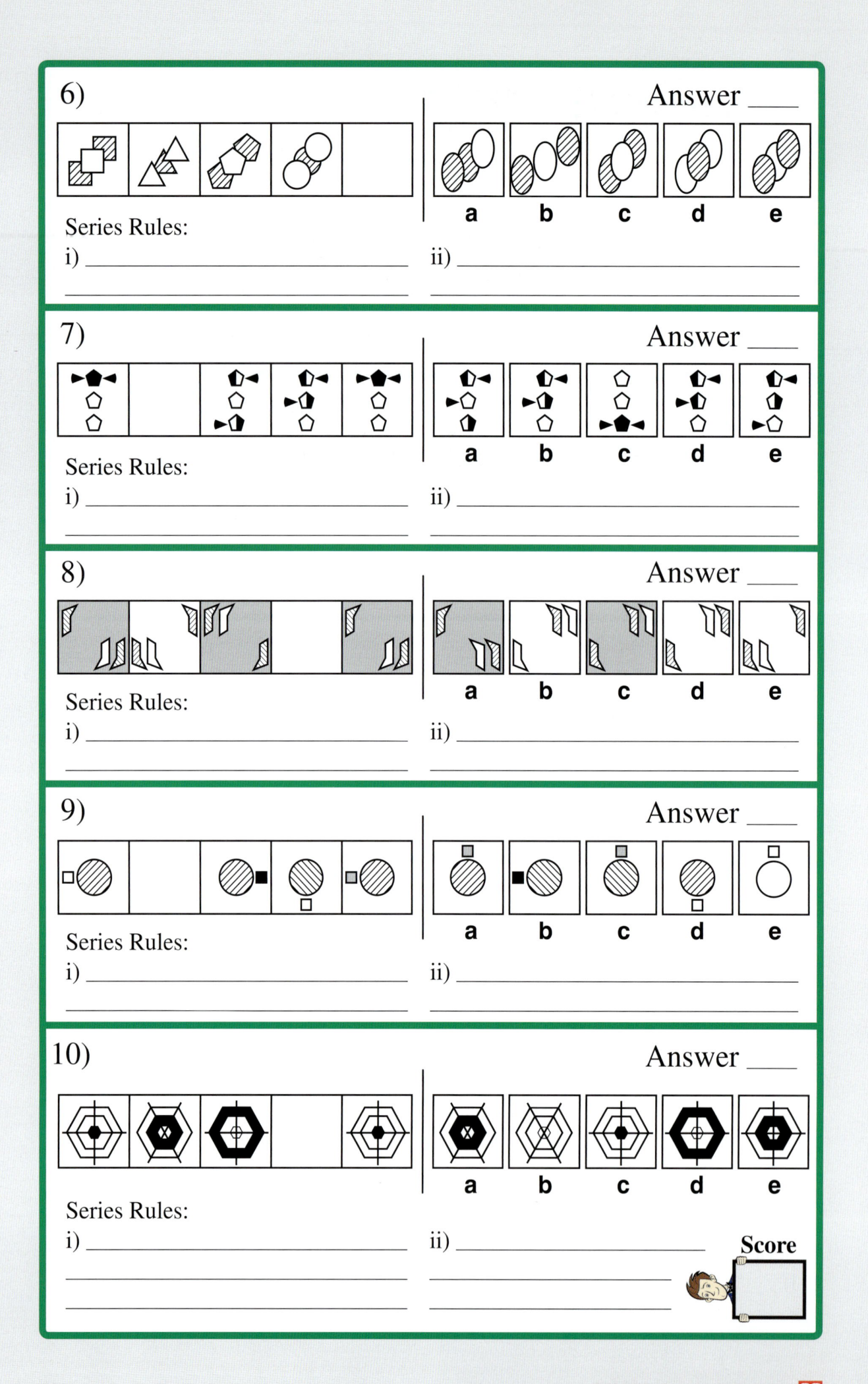

Series Rules:
i) _____   ii) _____

7) Answer ____

Series Rules:
i) _____   ii) _____

8) Answer ____

Series Rules:
i) _____   ii) _____

9) Answer ____

Series Rules:
i) _____   ii) _____

10) Answer ____

Series Rules:
i) _____   ii) _____

Score

52   © 2006 Stephen Curran

3. Level Three

In **Level Three** series questions, there are three layers or changes to look for in the sequence of shapes or figures.

Example: Which figure is missing in the series?

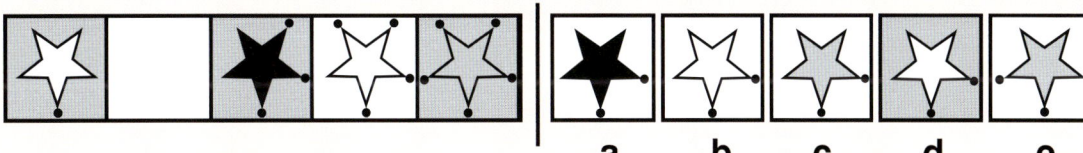

The Series Rules:

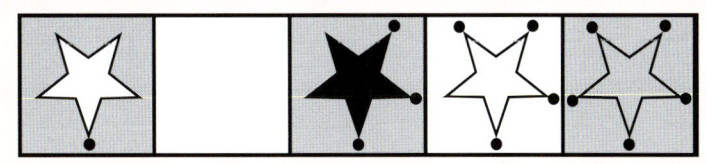

Layer 1 - The background fills in the squares alternate between Grey and White (repetitive pattern).
Layer 2 - The fills in the Star Shape go from White to Grey to Black to White, etc. (repetitive pattern).
Layer 3 - One Circle with a Black Fill is added at each stage in an anticlockwise direction around the Star Shape (cumulative pattern).

Remember: In series questions, a rule only occurs if it indicates something that changes as the series progresses, e.g. we do not need to say the main shape is always a Star.

The Set of Figures:

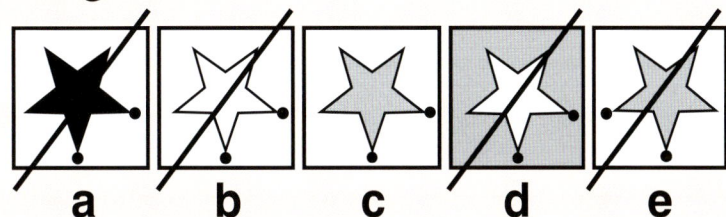

It is important to **eliminate** the wrong possibilities:
a - The Star Shape has a Black Fill.
b - The Star Shape has a White Fill.
d - The background fill is Grey and the Star Shape has a White Fill.
e - One Circle has been added in a clockwise direction.

The Correct Figure:

This figure follows the series rules.
Layer 1 - The background fill is White (repetitive).
Layer 2 - The Star Shape has a Grey Fill (repetitive).
Layer 3 - One Circle has been added in an anticlockwise direction around the shape (cumulative).

Answer: **c**

Exercise 11: 3

Which figure on the right completes the series on the left?

1) Series Rules:

i) The Circles must have a Grey Fill.

ii) The size sequence for the three central shapes is large, medium, small, etc.

iii) The Arrow rotates around the Square in an anticlockwise direction.

Answer ____

2) Series Rules:

i) _____

ii) _____

iii) _____

Answer ____

3) Series Rules:

i) _____

ii) _____

iii) _____

Answer ____

4) Series Rules:

i) _____

ii) _____

iii) _____

Answer ____

5) Series Rules:

i) _____

ii) _____

iii) _____

Answer ____

6) Series Rules:
   i) _____
   _____
   ii) _____   iii) _____

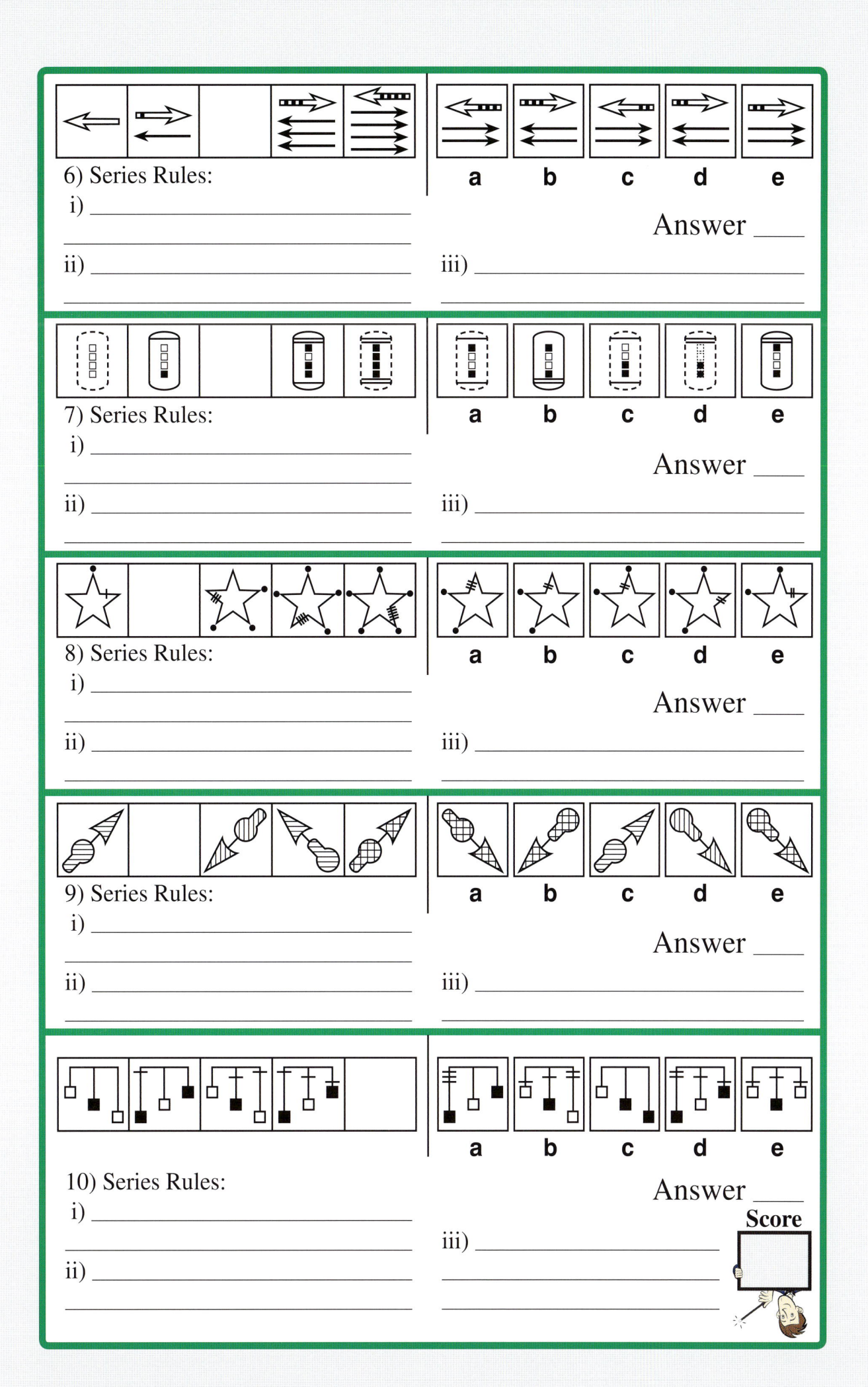

   Answer ____

7) Series Rules:
   i) _____
   _____
   ii) _____   iii) _____

   Answer ____

8) Series Rules:
   i) _____
   _____
   ii) _____   iii) _____

   Answer ____

9) Series Rules:
   i) _____
   _____
   ii) _____   iii) _____

   Answer ____

10) Series Rules:
    i) _____
    _____
    ii) _____   iii) _____

    Answer ____

    Score

© 2006 Stephen Curran

4. Levels Four & Five

In **Level Four** or **Five** series questions, there are four or five layers or changes to look for in the sequence of figures.

Example: Which figure is next in the series?

The Series Rules:

Layer 1 - The Arrowhead fill changes from White to Grey to Black (repetitive).
Layer 2 - The Arrow Shape rotates 90° Clockwise, excluding the fill (repetitive).
Layer 3 - The Rectangle fill is always Left Slant Shaded.
Layer 4 - The enclosed Kite Shape fill alternates from Black to White (repetitive).
Layer 5 - The Kite Shape rotates 180° each time within the Arrow Shape (repetitive).

Remember: In series questions, a rule only occurs if it indicates something that changes as the series progresses, e.g. we do not need to say the outer shape is always an Arrow.

The Set of Figures:

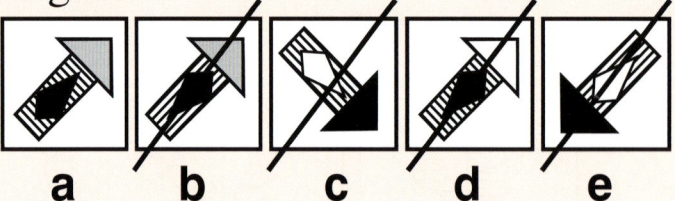

It is important to **eliminate** the wrong possibilities:

b - The Rectangle fill is Right Slant Shaded and the enclosed Kite Shape is the wrong way up.
c - The Arrow Shape is facing the wrong way and the enclosed Kite Shape has a White Fill. The Arrowhead fill is also Black.
d - The Arrowhead fill is White and the enclosed Kite Shape is the wrong way up.
e - The Arrow Shape is facing the wrong way, the Arrowhead fill is Black, the Rectangle fill is Right Slant Shaded and the enclosed Kite Shape has a White Fill and is the wrong way up.

The Correct Figure:

The figure follows the series rules.
Layer 1 - The Arrowhead fill is Grey (repetitive).
Layer 2 - The Arrow Shape points the right way (repetitive).
Layer 3 - The Rectangle fill is Left Slant Shaded.
Layer 4 - The enclosed Kite Shape fill is Black.
Answer: **a**   **Layer 5** - The enclosed Kite Shape is the right way up.

Exercise 11: 4

Which figure on the right completes the series on the left?

1) Series Rules: Answer _____

i) One Cross Shape is added at each stage.

ii) One Square with a White Fill is added at each stage.

iii) One Hexagon is added at each stage.

iv) The Hexagon fill alternates Black, White, Black, White, etc.

2) Series Rules: Answer _____

i) _____

ii) _____

iii) _____

iv) _____

3) Series Rules: Answer _____

i) _____

ii) _____

iii) _____

iv) _____

4) Series Rules: Answer _____

i) _____

ii) _____

iii) _____

iv) _____

5) Series Rules: Answer _____

i) _____

ii) _____

iii) _____

iv) _____

© 2006 Stephen Curran

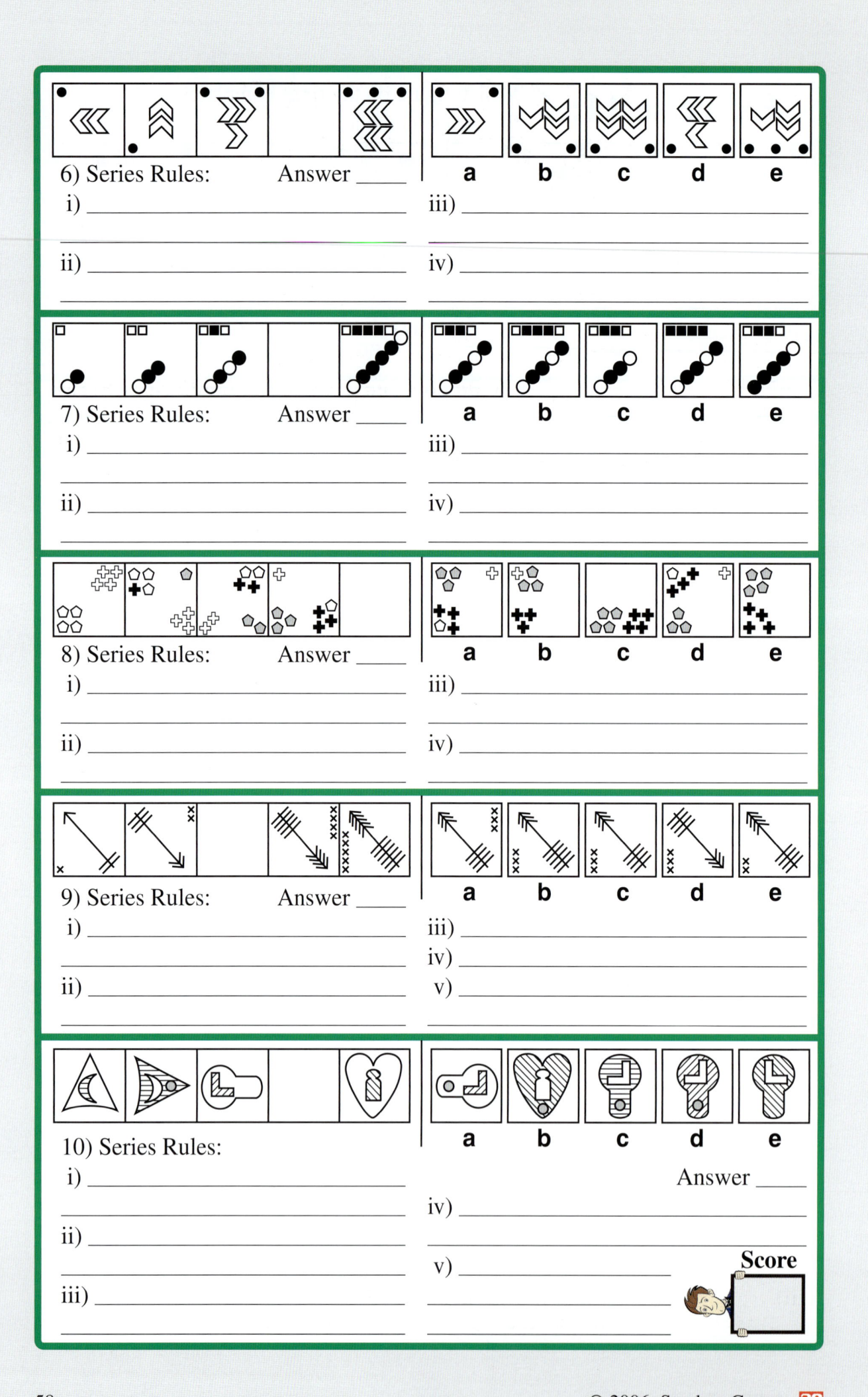

6) Series Rules: Answer ____
    i) _____
    ii) _____
    iii) _____
    iv) _____

   a   b   c   d   e

7) Series Rules: Answer ____
    i) _____
    ii) _____
    iii) _____
    iv) _____

   a   b   c   d   e

8) Series Rules: Answer ____
    i) _____
    ii) _____
    iii) _____
    iv) _____

   a   b   c   d   e

9) Series Rules: Answer ____
    i) _____
    ii) _____
    iii) _____
    iv) _____
    v) _____

   a   b   c   d   e

10) Series Rules:
    i) _____
    ii) _____
    iii) _____
    iv) _____
    v) _____

   a   b   c   d   e

   Answer ____

   Score

58 © 2006 Stephen Curran

Chapter Twelve
MATRICES

Matrices occur in mathematics rather than Verbal Reasoning.

For example: This matrix adds up to **30** in every direction: horizontally, vertically and diagonally.

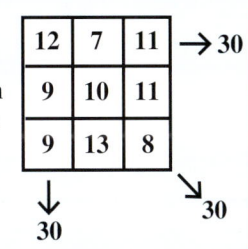

12	7	11	→ 30
9	10	11	
9	13	8	

↓ 30 ↘ 30

Matrices are able to test all the key Non-verbal Reasoning skills needed to identify:

Similarity • **Difference** • **Pattern**

A matrix can combine these other question types:

Odd One Out • **Analogy** • **Similarity** • **Series**

1. Level One

In **Level One** matrix questions, there is only one layer or change to look for. Matrix questions are of two types:

1) A Four Square Matrix.

Example: Which shape should fill the empty square?

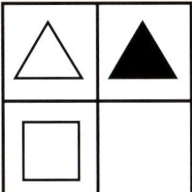

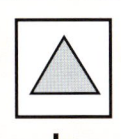

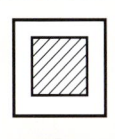

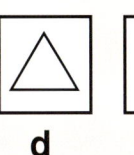

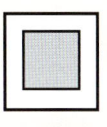

Answer: **a**

Four Square Matrices are **analogies** and can work horizontally, vertically and diagonally. This matrix analogy works both horizontally and vertically.

Horizontal - Triangle with a White Fill to Triangle with a Black Fill.
- Square with a White Fill to Square with a Black Fill.

Vertical - Triangle with a White Fill to Square with a White Fill.
- Triangle with a Black Fill to Square with a Black Fill.

2) A Nine Square Matrix.

Example: Which shape should fill the empty square?

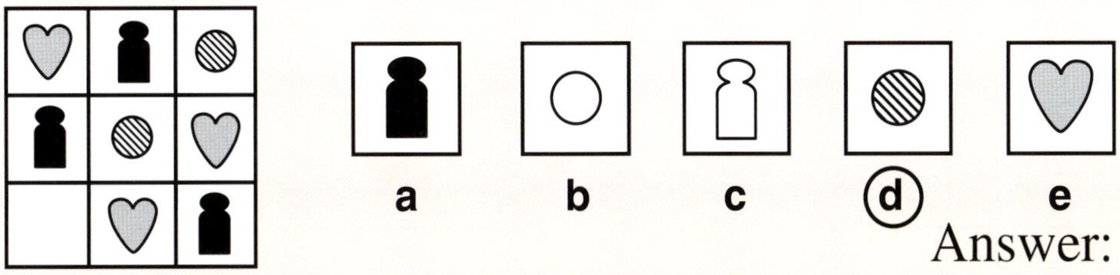

Answer: **d**

This Nine Square Matrix works as a **series** or **pattern**.
Each column and row must have all three shapes: Heart, Churn, Circle.
The Circles with shaded fills lie along a right slant diagonal line.

© 2006 Stephen Curran

Exercise 12: 1

Which shape or figure on the right completes the matrix on the left?

1) Matrix Rule:
Horizontal: The fill changes from White to Vertical Shaded
or Vertical: The Heptagon becomes a Square.

Answer ____

2) Matrix Rule: ____

Answer ____

3) Matrix Rule: ____

Answer ____

4) Matrix Rule: ____

Answer ____

5) Matrix Rule: ____

Answer ____

60 © 2006 Stephen Curran

6) Matrix Rule: _____

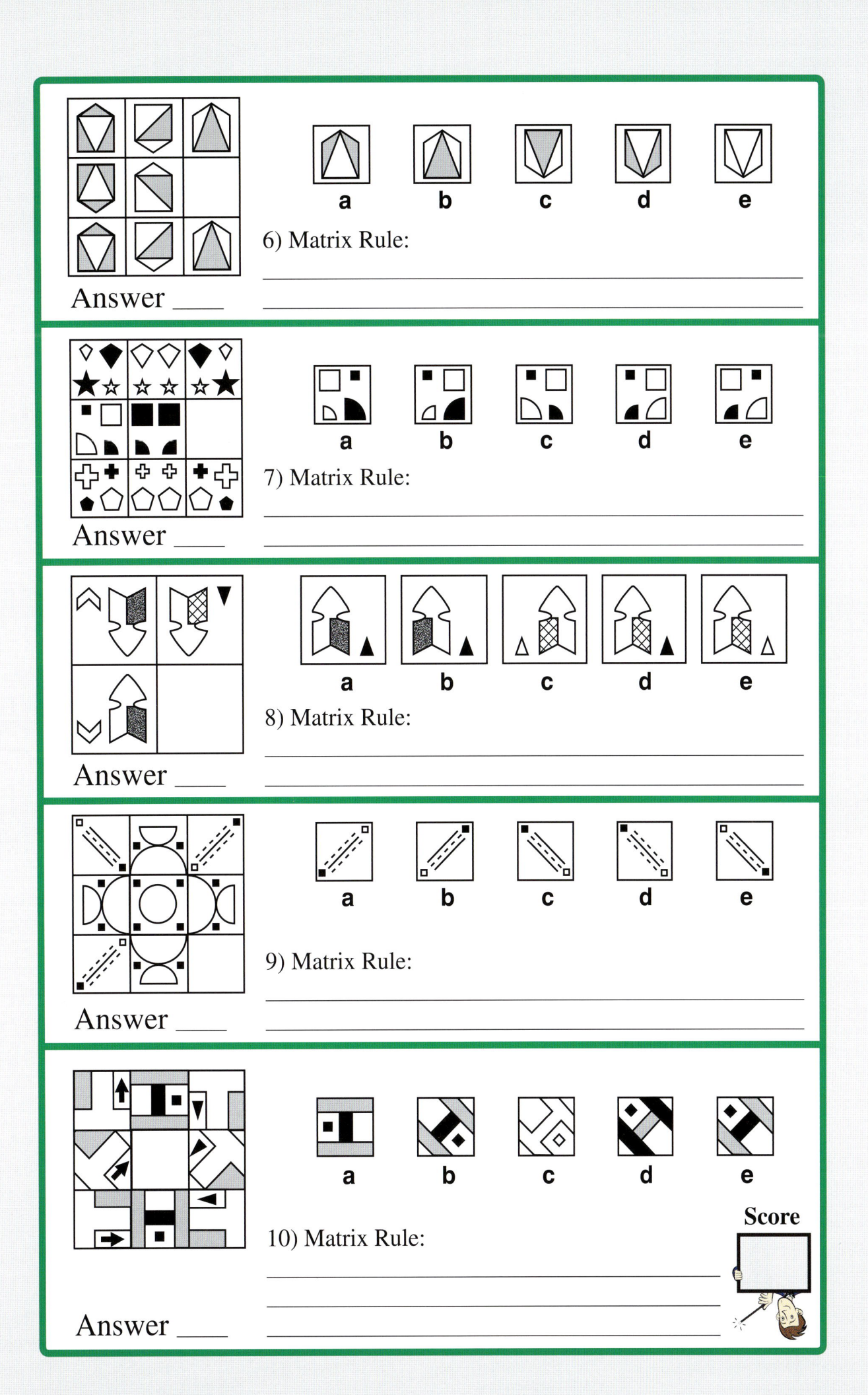

Answer ____

7) Matrix Rule: _____

Answer ____

8) Matrix Rule: _____

Answer ____

9) Matrix Rule: _____

Answer ____

10) Matrix Rule: _____

Answer ____

Score

© 2006 Stephen Curran

61

2. Level Two

In **Level Two** matrix questions, there are two layers or changes to look for between the shapes or figures.

Example: Which figure should fill the empty square?

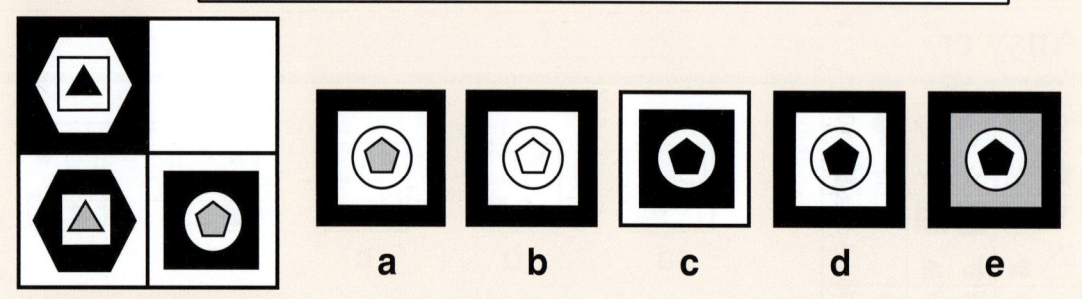

The Matrix Rules: This matrix analogy works horizontally and vertically (by row and by column). However these rules are best established vertically (upwards) as the shapes are of the same type.

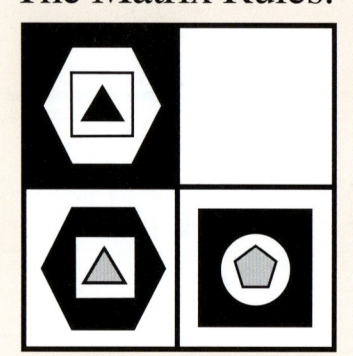

Layer 1 - The fills of the outer two shapes reverse: Black goes to White, White goes to Black.

Layer 2 - The Grey Fill in the smallest enclosed shape becomes Black.

Note: If the shapes in either a row or column are of the same type, it is best to establish the rules in that direction.

The Set of Figures:

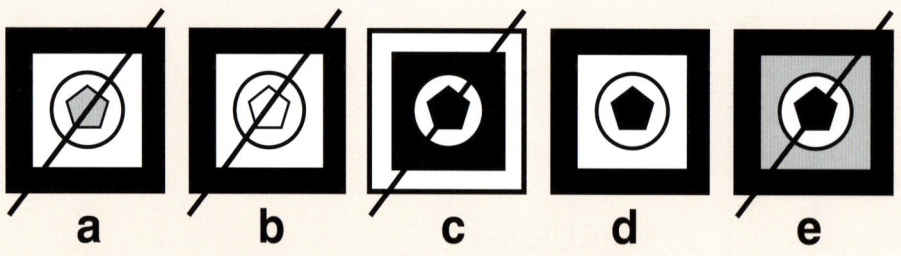

It is important to **eliminate** the wrong possibilities:

a - The Pentagon has a Grey Fill.
b - The Pentagon has a White Fill.
c - The fills of the two outer shapes have not been reversed.
e - The fills of the two outer shapes have not been reversed.

The Correct Figure:

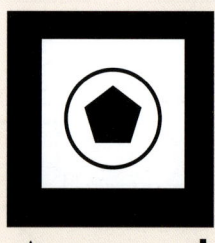

The matrix follows the analogy rules.

Layer 1 - The fills of the two outer shapes reverse: Black goes to White and White goes to Black.

Layer 2 - The Grey Fill in the Pentagon becomes Black.

Answer: **d**

Exercise 12: 2   Which shape or figure on the right completes the matrix?

Note: If the shapes in a row or column are of the same type, establish the rules in that direction.

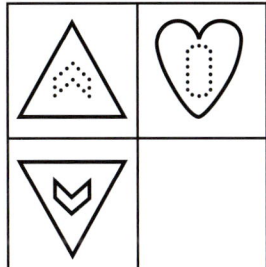

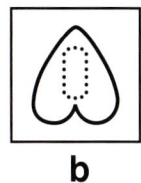

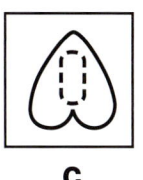

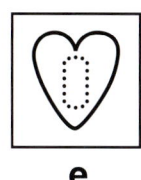

1) Matrix Rules: This matrix is best solved _vertically_.
   i) The whole figure reflects.
   ii) The Dotted Line of the enclosed shape becomes solid.

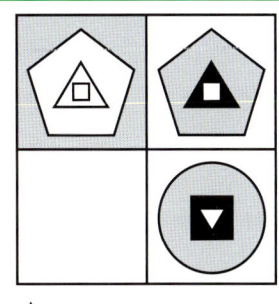

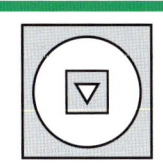

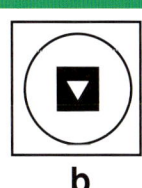

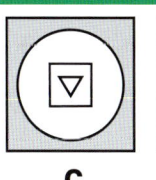

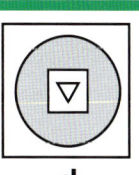

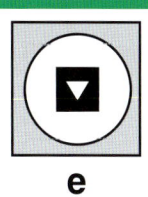

Answer ____

2) Matrix Rules: This matrix is best solved _horizontally_.
   i) _____
   ii) _____

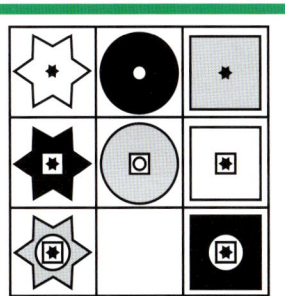

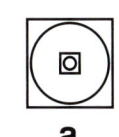

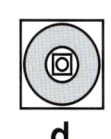

Answer ____

3) Matrix Rules: This matrix is best solved _____.
   i) _____
   ii) _____

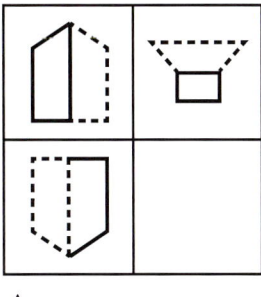

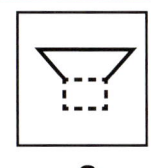

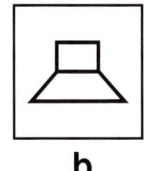

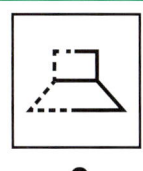

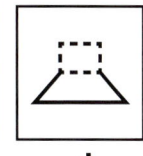

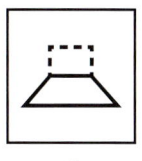

Answer ____

4) Matrix Rules: This matrix is best solved _____.
   i) _____
   ii) _____

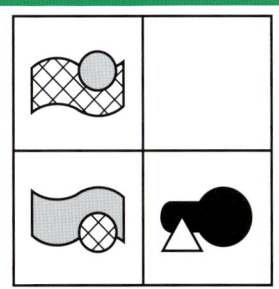

Answer ____

5) Matrix Rules: This matrix is best solved _____.
   i) _____
   ii) _____

Answer ____

© 2006 Stephen Curran

63

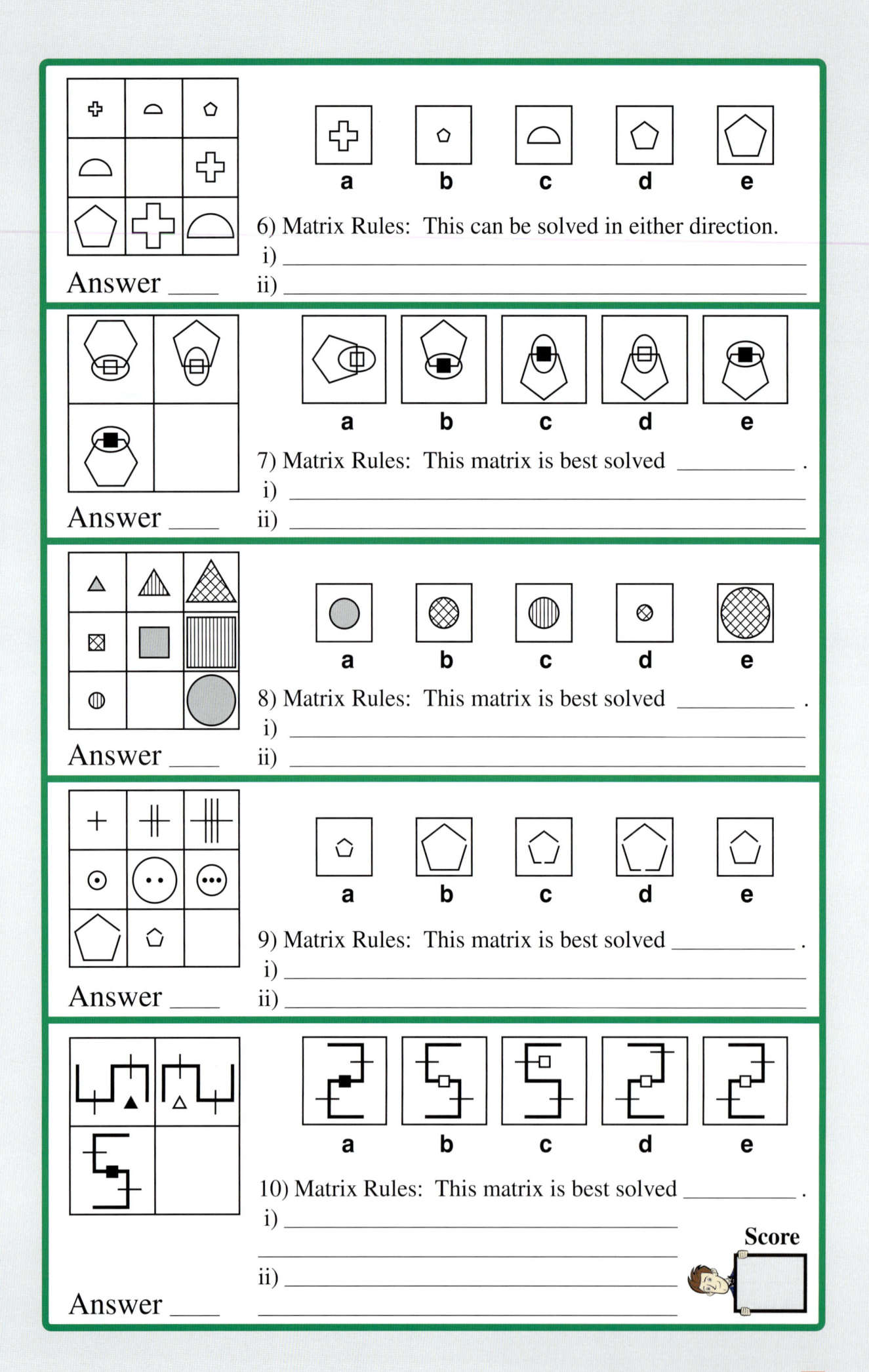

6) Matrix Rules: This can be solved in either direction.
   i) _____
   ii) _____

Answer ____

7) Matrix Rules: This matrix is best solved _____ .
   i) _____
   ii) _____

Answer ____

8) Matrix Rules: This matrix is best solved _____ .
   i) _____
   ii) _____

Answer ____

9) Matrix Rules: This matrix is best solved _____ .
   i) _____
   ii) _____

Answer ____

10) Matrix Rules: This matrix is best solved _____ .
    i) _____
    ii) _____

Answer ____

Score

64 © 2006 Stephen Curran

3. Level Three

In **Level Three** matrix questions, there are three layers or changes to look for between the shapes or figures.

Example: Which figure should fill the empty square?

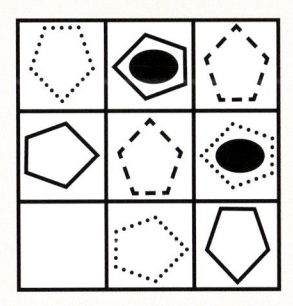

The Matrix Rules: 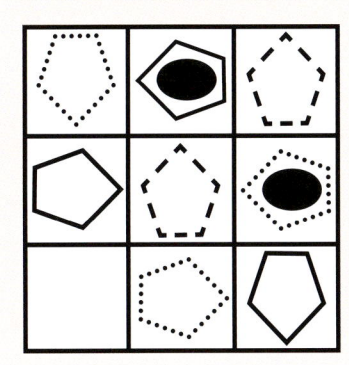 This matrix can be solved horizontally or vertically.

Layer 1 - The Irregular Pentagon is rotated 90° clockwise or anticlockwise by row and by column.

Layer 2 - There must be one enclosed Ellipse in each row and column.

Layer 3 - There must be one of each line type in each row and column: Dotted, Dashed and Solid.

Remember: If the shapes in either a row or column are of the same type, establish the rules in that direction.

The Set of Figures:

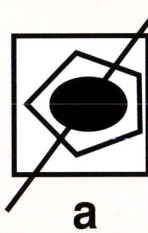

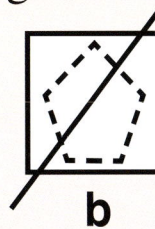

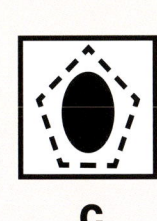

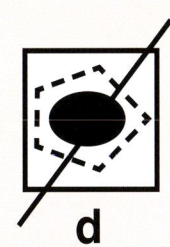

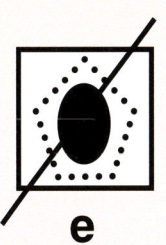

It is important to **eliminate** the wrong possibilities:

a - The figure is facing the wrong way and has the incorrect line type.
b - There is no Ellipse.
d - The figure is facing the wrong way.
e - The shape has the incorrect line type.

The Correct Figure:

The matrix follows the pattern rules.

Layer 1 - The Irregular Pentagon is pointing in the right direction (at a 90° rotation to the other two shapes).
Layer 2 - There is an enclosed Ellipse.
Layer 3 - The Irregular Pentagon has a Dashed Line.

Answer: **c**

Exercise 12: 3

Which shape or figure on the right completes the matrix?

Note: If the shapes in a row or column are of the same type, establish the rules in that direction.

1) Matrix Rules: This matrix is best solved _horizontally_.
   i) Each row has alternating large and small figures.
   ii) Each row has one of each fill type: Grey, White, Shaded.
   iii) Lines across small shapes run the same way as the shading.

Answer ____

2) Matrix Rules: This matrix is best solved _vertically_.
   i) ____
   ii) ____
   iii) ____

Answer ____

3) Matrix Rules: This matrix is best solved ____.
   i) ____
   ii) ____
   iii) ____

Answer ____

4) Matrix Rules: This matrix is best solved ____.
   i) ____
   ii) ____
   iii) ____

Answer ____

5) Matrix Rules: This matrix is best solved ____.
   i) ____
   ii) ____
   iii) ____

Answer ____

© 2006 Stephen Curran

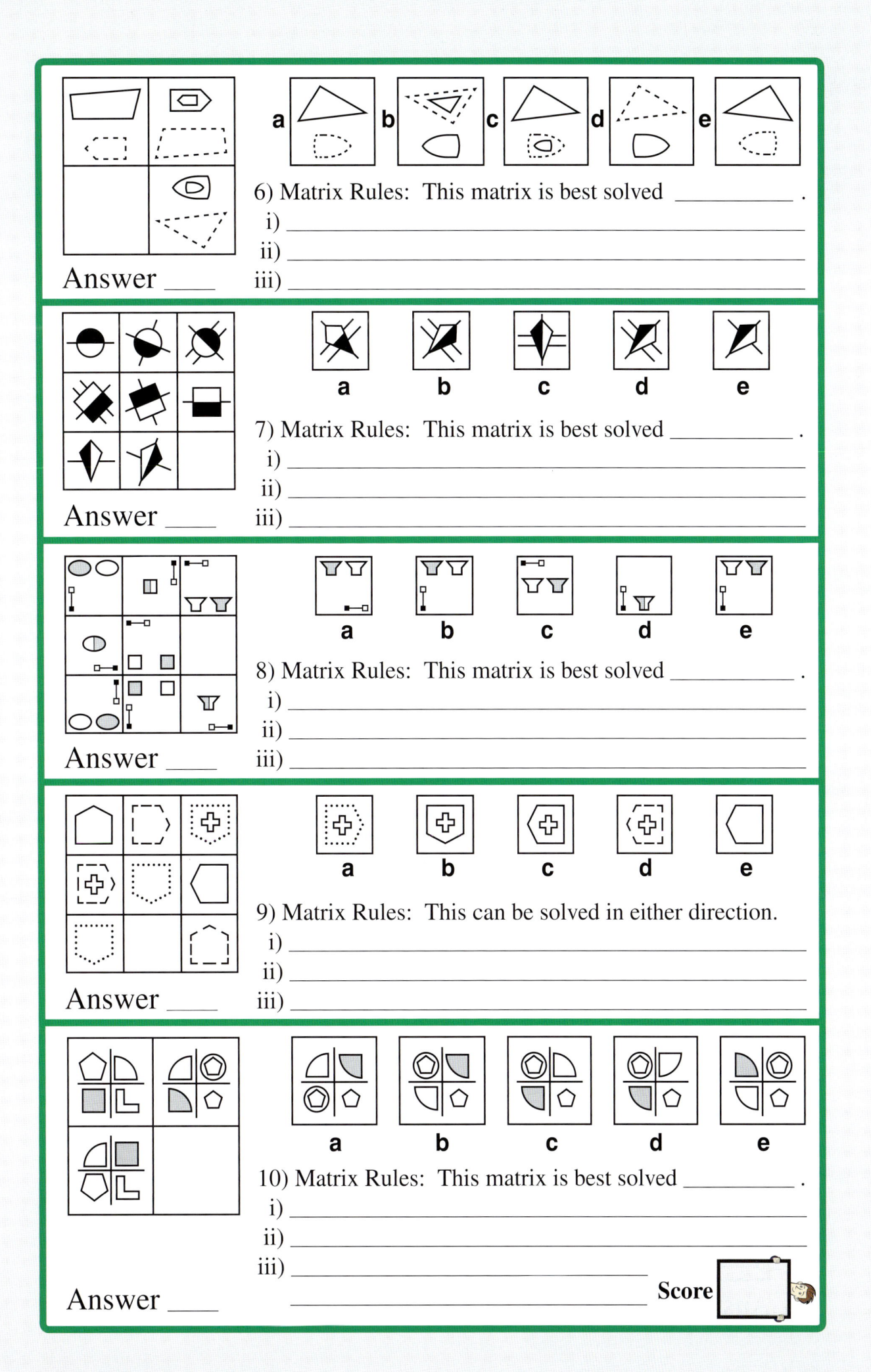

6) Matrix Rules: This matrix is best solved _____.
   i) _____
   ii) _____
   iii) _____
Answer ____

7) Matrix Rules: This matrix is best solved _____.
   i) _____
   ii) _____
   iii) _____
Answer ____

8) Matrix Rules: This matrix is best solved _____.
   i) _____
   ii) _____
   iii) _____
Answer ____

9) Matrix Rules: This can be solved in either direction.
   i) _____
   ii) _____
   iii) _____
Answer ____

10) Matrix Rules: This matrix is best solved _____.
   i) _____
   ii) _____
   iii) _____
Answer ____

Score [ ]

© 2006 Stephen Curran

4. Levels Four & Five

In **Level Four** or **Five** matrix questions, there are four or five layers or changes to look for between the shapes or figures.

Example: Which figure should fill the empty square?

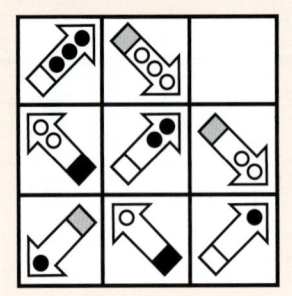

The Matrix Rules:

This matrix works horizontally and vertically.

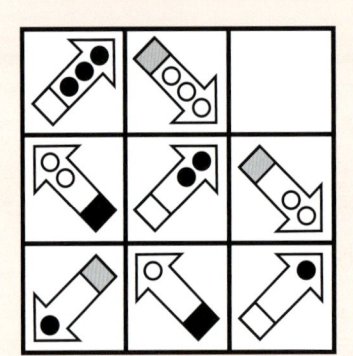

Layer 1 - The Arrow Shapes are rotated at 90° to each other at each stage.
Layer 2 - The Arrow Shapes have either 1, 2 or 3 enclosed Circles. Each row has the same number of Circles and each column has 1, 2 and 3 Circles.
Layer 3 - The enclosed Rectangles in each row and column have different fills: White, Grey or Black.
Layer 4 - The Circles must have alternate Black and White Fills in each row and column.

Remember: If the shapes in either a row or column are of the same type, establish the rules in that direction.

The Set of Figures:

It is important to **eliminate** the wrong possibilities:

a - There are only two enclosed Circles.
c - The Rectangle and Circle fills are incorrect.
d - The Arrow Shape points in the wrong direction.
e - The Circle fills are incorrect.

The Correct Figure:

The matrix follows the pattern rules.

Layer 1 - The Arrow Shape points in the right direction.
Layer 2 - There are three enclosed Circles.
Layer 3 - The enclosed Rectangle has a Black Fill.
Layer 4 - The Enclosed Circles have Black Fills.

Answer: **b**

Exercise 12: 4
Which figure on the right completes the matrix?

1) Matrix Rules: This can be solved in either direction.
  i) Arrow Shapes are rotated 90° by row and 180° by column.
  ii) One of each Square fill type by row/column: Black, Grey, White.
  iii) Number of Squares: 1, 2, 3 by column; same number in each row.
  iv) By row/column: The Arrow has 0, 1, 2 extra Lines in any order.

Answer ____

2) Matrix Rules: This matrix is best solved _horizontally_.
  i) _____
  ii) _____
  iii) _____
  iv) _____

Answer ____

3) Matrix Rules: This matrix is best solved _vertically_.
  i) _____
  ii) _____
  iii) _____
  iv) _____

Answer ____

4) Matrix Rules: This matrix is best solved _____.
  i) _____
  ii) _____
  iii) _____
  iv) _____

Answer ____

5) Matrix Rules: This matrix is best solved _____.
  i) _____
  ii) _____
  iii) _____
  iv) _____

Answer ____

© 2006 Stephen Curran

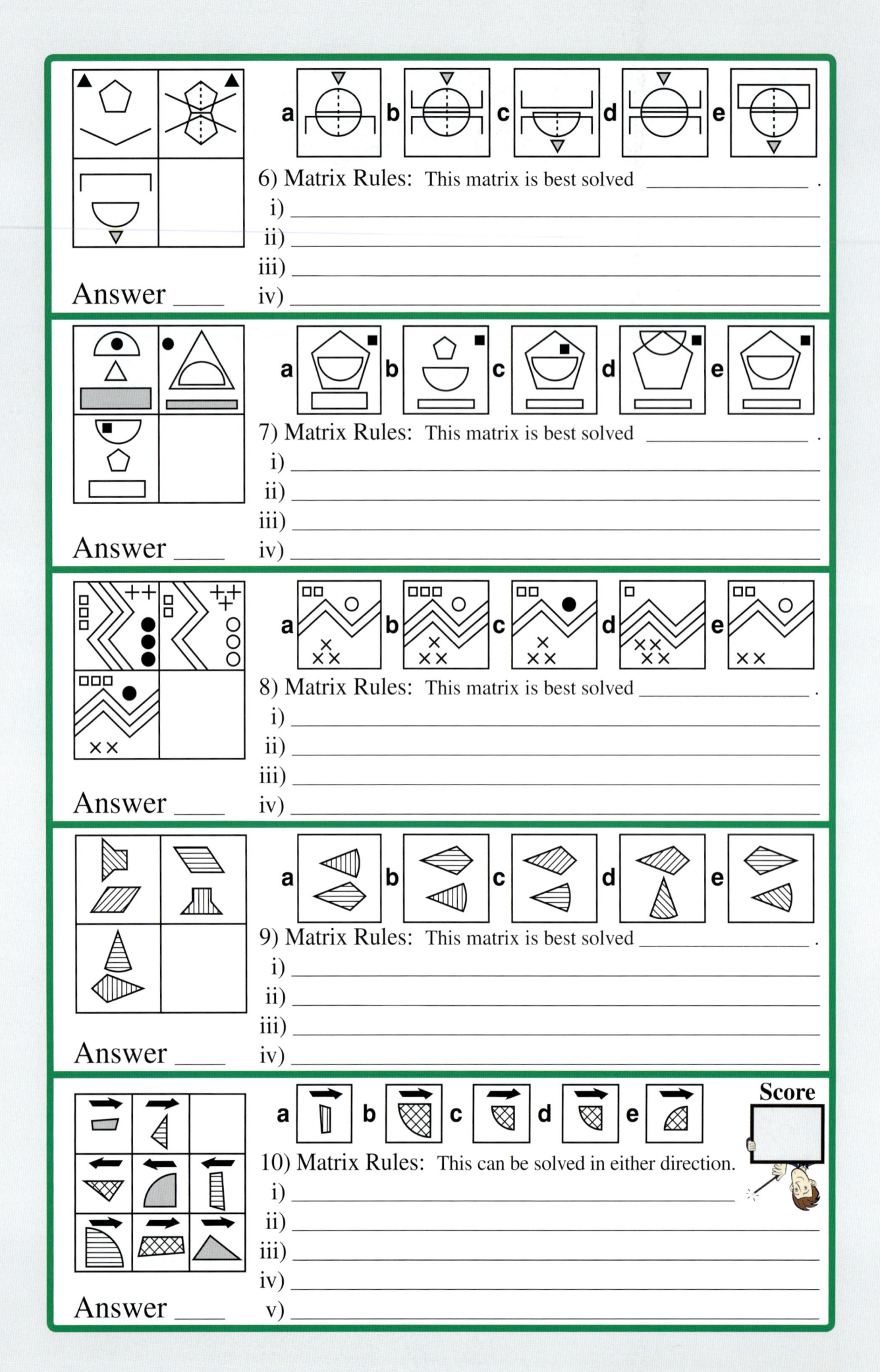

6) Matrix Rules: This matrix is best solved _____ .
   i) _____
   ii) _____
   iii) _____
   iv) _____

Answer ____

7) Matrix Rules: This matrix is best solved _____ .
   i) _____
   ii) _____
   iii) _____
   iv) _____

Answer ____

8) Matrix Rules: This matrix is best solved _____ .
   i) _____
   ii) _____
   iii) _____
   iv) _____

Answer ____

9) Matrix Rules: This matrix is best solved _____ .
   i) _____
   ii) _____
   iii) _____
   iv) _____

Answer ____

10) Matrix Rules: This can be solved in either direction.
   i) _____
   ii) _____
   iii) _____
   iv) _____
   v) _____

Answer ____

Score

70 © 2006 Stephen Curran

Chapter Thirteen
REVISION

1. Odd One Out

Exercise 13: 1a Which figure is the odd one out?

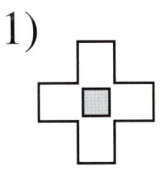

1) a b c d e

Answer ____

2) a b c d e

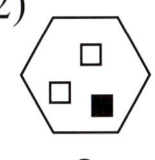

Answer ____

3) a b c d e

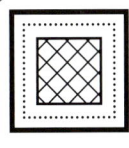

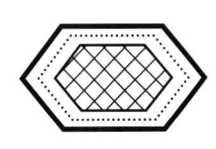

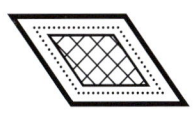

Answer ____

4) a b c d e

Answer ____

5) a b c d e

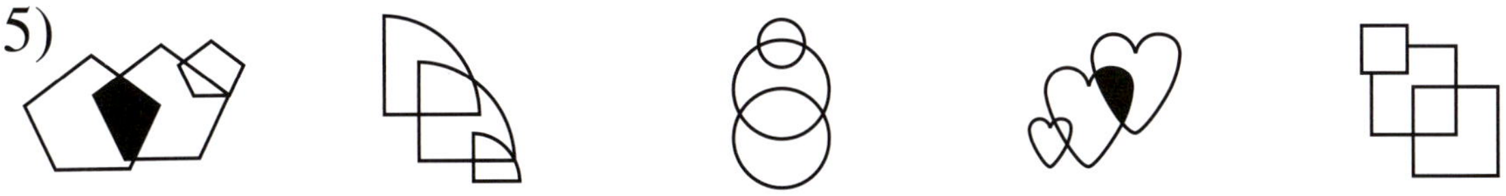

Answer ____

2. Codes

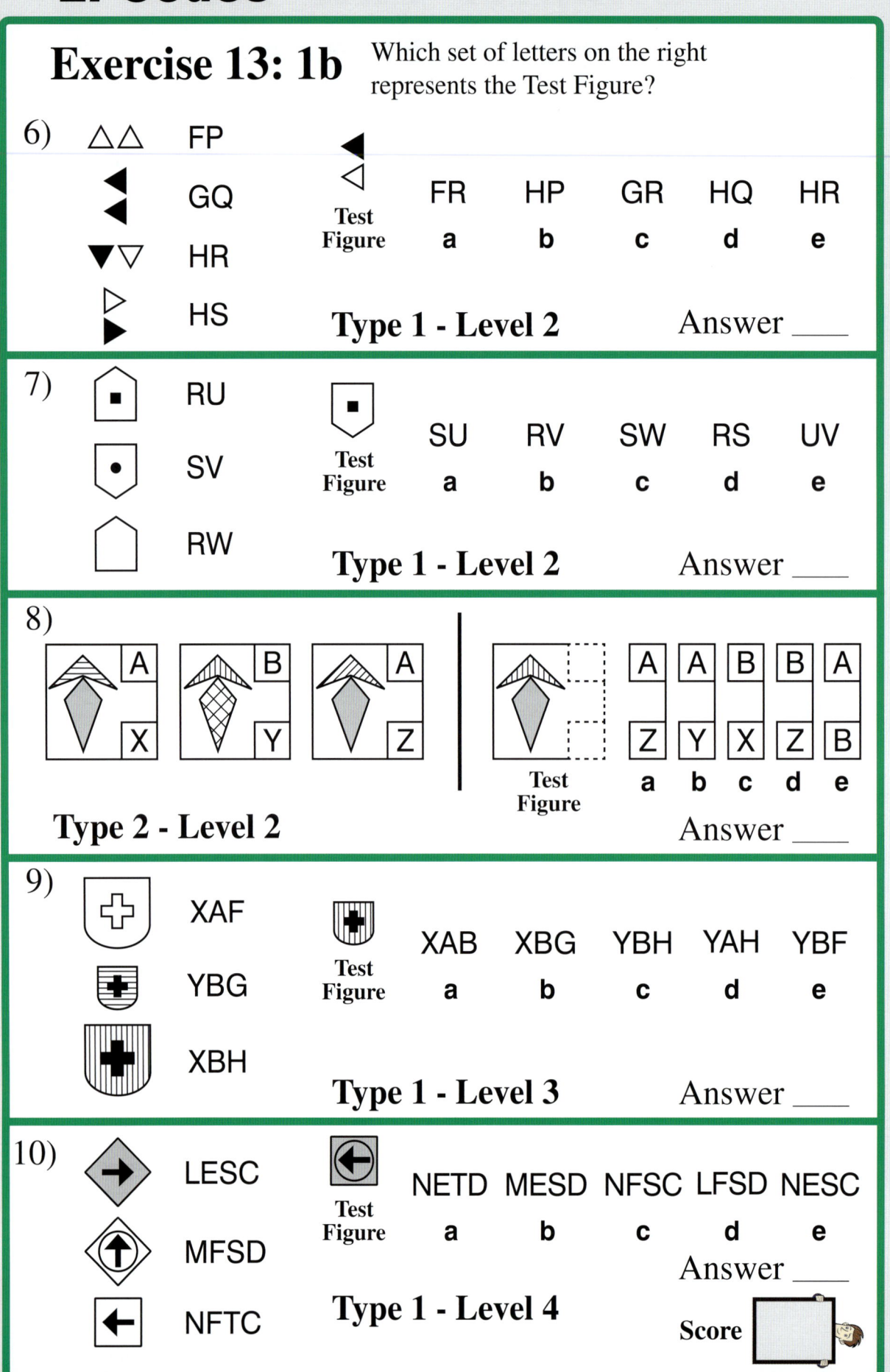

Exercise 13: 1b Which set of letters on the right represents the Test Figure?

6)

△△	FP	
◀◀	GQ	
▼▽	HR	
▷▪	HS	

Test Figure: ◀ / ◁

FR	HP	GR	HQ	HR
a	b	c	d	e

Type 1 - Level 2   Answer ____

7)

⬠■	RU
⬠•	SV
⬠	RW

Test Figure: ⬠■

SU	RV	SW	RS	UV
a	b	c	d	e

Type 1 - Level 2   Answer ____

8)

A / X, B / Y, A / Z

Test Figure

A/Z	A/Y	B/X	B/Z	A/B
a	b	c	d	e

Type 2 - Level 2   Answer ____

9)

shield +	XAF
shield +	YBG
shield +	XBH

Test Figure

XAB	XBG	YBH	YAH	YBF
a	b	c	d	e

Type 1 - Level 3   Answer ____

10)

→	LESC
↑	MFSD
←	NFTC

Test Figure: ←

NETD	MESD	NFSC	LFSD	NESC
a	b	c	d	e

Type 1 - Level 4   Answer ____

Score ____

3. Analogy

Exercise 13: 2a Which shape or figure completes the analogy?

1)

Level 1 Answer ____

2)

Level 2 Answer ____

3)

Level 3 Answer ____

4)

Level 4 Answer ____

5)

Level 5 Answer ____

© 2006 Stephen Curran

4. Similarities

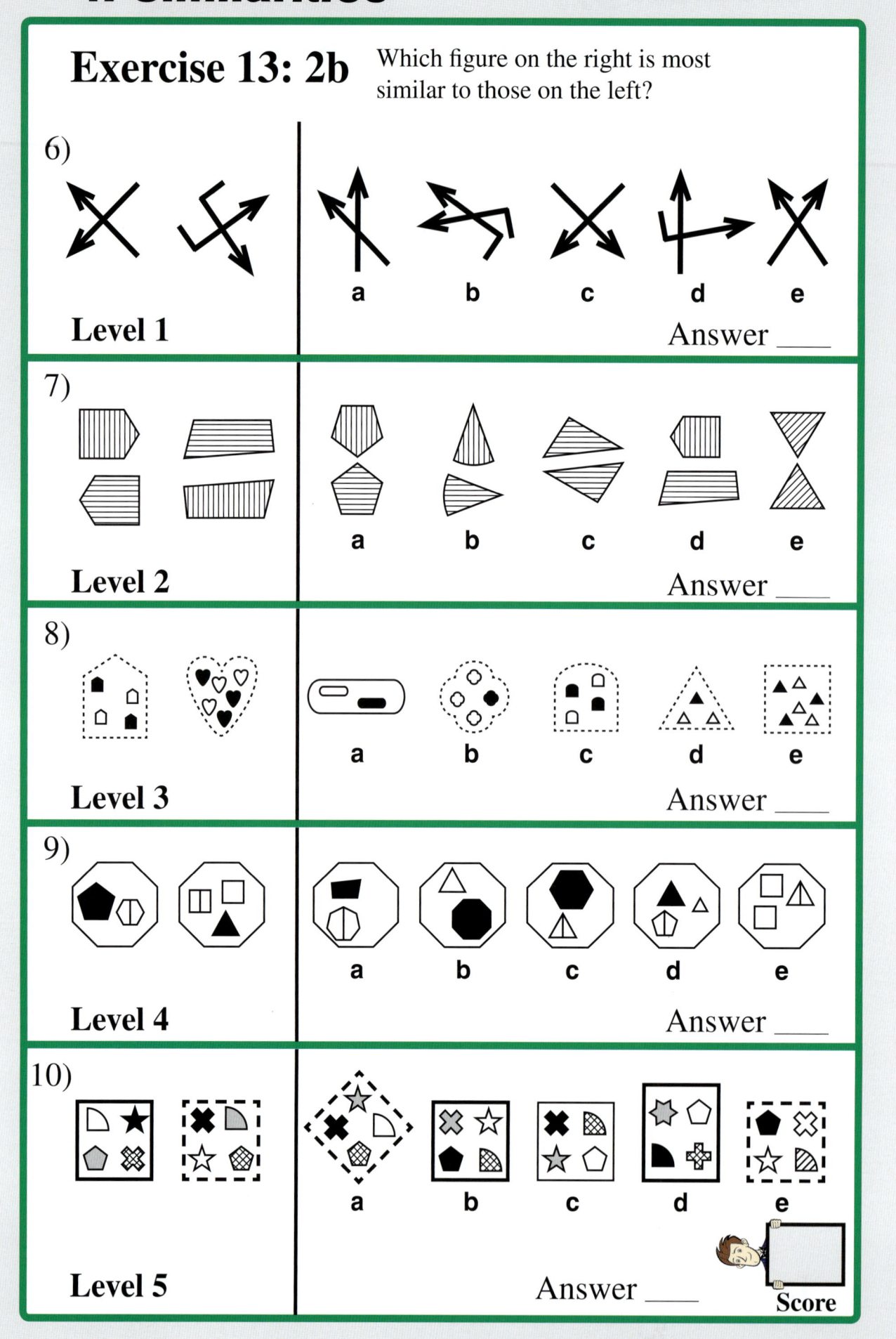

Exercise 13: 2b — Which figure on the right is most similar to those on the left?

6) **Level 1**

a b c d e

Answer ____

7) **Level 2**

a b c d e

Answer ____

8) **Level 3**

a b c d e

Answer ____

9) **Level 4**

a b c d e

Answer ____

10) **Level 5**

a b c d e

Answer ____ Score

74 © 2006 Stephen Curran

5. Series

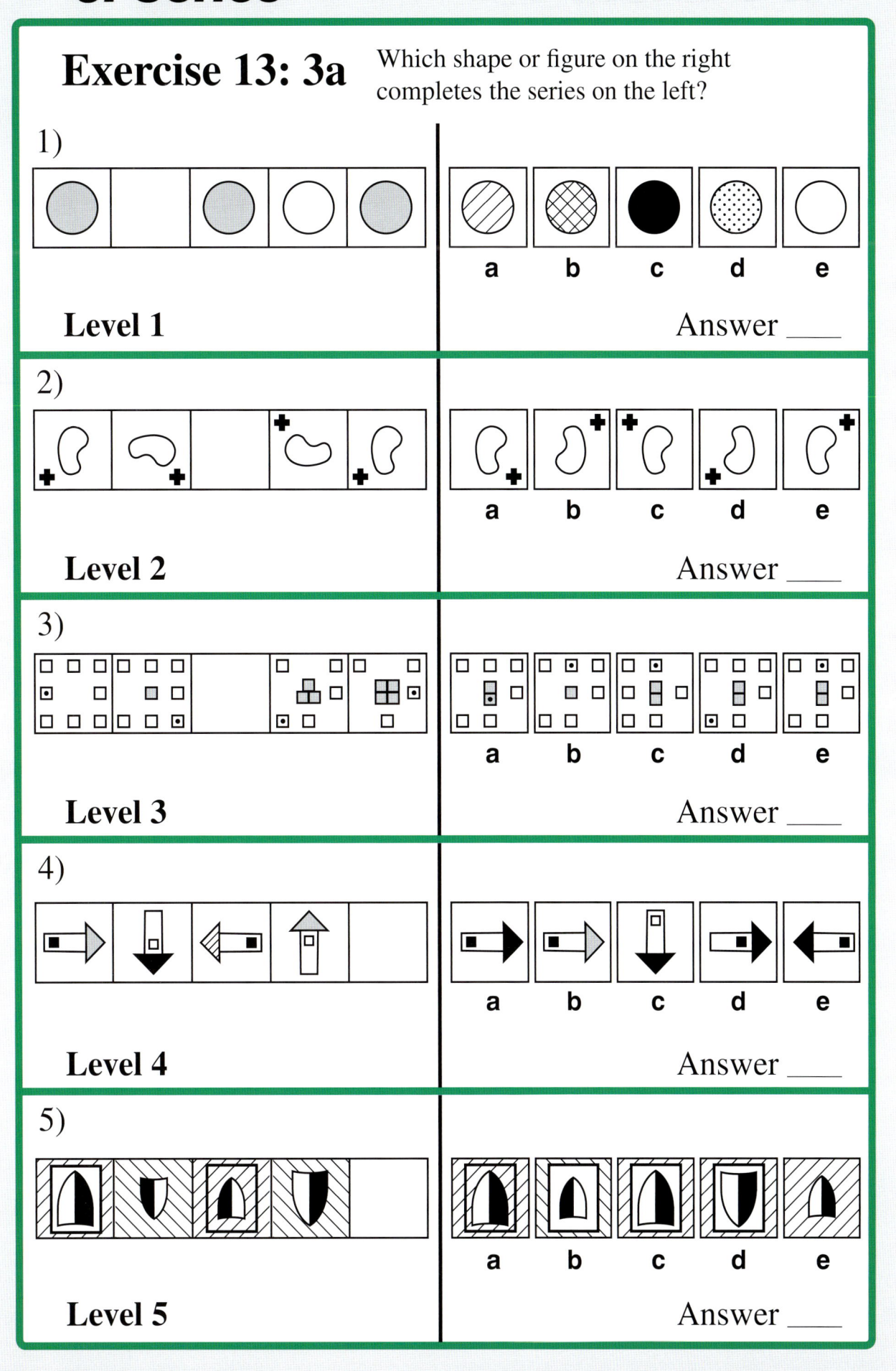

Exercise 13: 3a

Which shape or figure on the right completes the series on the left?

1)

a b c d e

Level 1 Answer ____

2)

a b c d e

Level 2 Answer ____

3)

a b c d e

Level 3 Answer ____

4)

a b c d e

Level 4 Answer ____

5)

a b c d e

Level 5 Answer ____

© 2006 Stephen Curran

6. Matrices

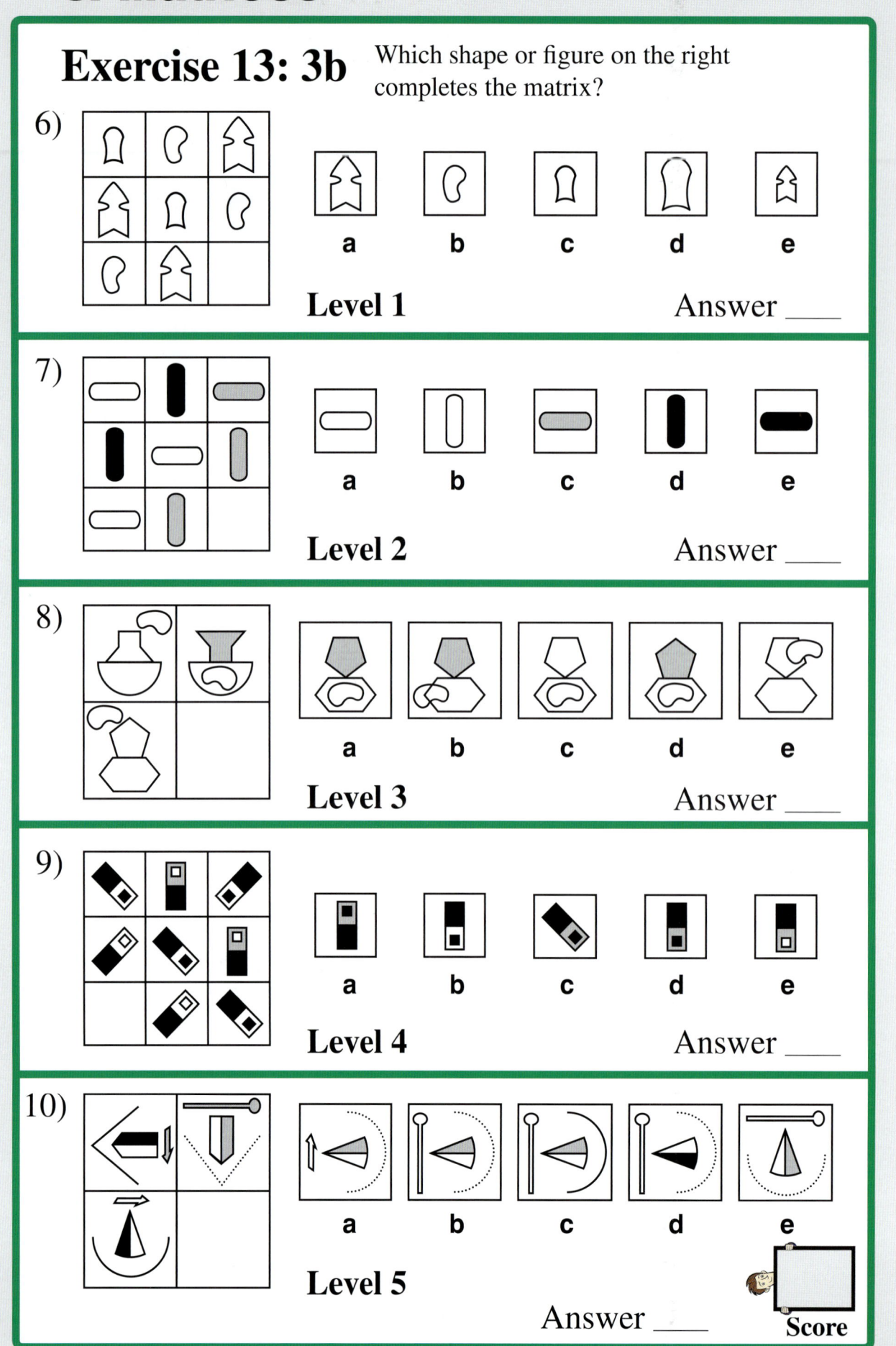

Exercise 13: 3b
Which shape or figure on the right completes the matrix?

6)

a b c d e

Level 1 Answer ____

7)

a b c d e

Level 2 Answer ____

8)

a b c d e

Level 3 Answer ____

9)

a b c d e

Level 4 Answer ____

10)

a b c d e

Level 5

Answer ____ **Score**

76 © 2006 Stephen Curran

11+ Non-verbal Reasoning Year 5-7 Workbook 2

Answers

Chapter Seven
Odd One Out
Exercise 7: 1

1) **c** - The Triangle is smaller than the other Triangles.
2) **b** - It is the only figure with four Black Fill Circles or the only figure with a Black Fill Circle at the bottom.
3) **c** - One small shape has not been overlayed onto the bigger shape.
4) **e** - If the figure is rotated to match the other figures, the shading will slant the wrong way.
5) **e** - The figure has been divided into four parts instead of three parts.
6) **b** - The central Square merges with the Diagonal Lines.
7) **e** - The Cross Shapes should number one more than the Squares.
8) **d** - It is the only shape that points in a downward direction.
9) **a** - The figure rotates in a different direction (an inversion of the other figures).
10) **c** - The frequency (number) of both sets of Lines within the figure is the same.

Exercise 7: 2

1) **a** - The two Segment Shapes inside the Circle are different from those in the other Circles.
2) **c** - The Circle with the Black Fill must be enclosed within the Pentagon.
3) **c** - It is the only figure where the Segment Shape has a Grey Fill.
4) **e** - It is the only figure which has 3 enclosed Star Shapes.
5) **d** - It is the only figure where both shapes have the same fill.
6) **b** - The figure has been flipped or inverted instead of being rotated.
7) **a** - It is the only figure where the large shape has a Horizontally Shaded Fill.
8) **c** - The outer shape is a Pentagon and not a Hexagon.
9) **e** - The Thick Solid Line crosses the Flower Shape at a different place from the other Flower Shapes.
10) **c** - The 2 Cross Shapes are adjacent rather than on opposite sides of the Quadrilateral.

Chapter Eight
Codes
Exercise 8: 1

1) **b**
   i) R - Small Squares; Q - Large Squares.
   ii) L - Right Slant Shaded Fill; J - Lattice Fill.
2) **c**
   i) M - Black Fills; N - White Fills.
   ii) A - Two Circles; B - Three Circles.
3) **e**
   i) T - Arrow pointing left; S - Arrow pointing upwards.
   ii) G - White Fills; F - Right Slant Shaded Fill.
4) **a**
   i) X - Small Octagon; Y - Large Octagon.
   ii) B - Vertical Shading; A - Horizontal Shading.
5) **c**
   i) Q - White Fill; P - Lattice Fill.
   ii) C - Star; D - Speaker.
6) **d**
   i) J, K and L - Three Quadrants rotated differently.
   ii) W - Circle with White Fill; X - Circle with Black Fill.
7) **e**
   i) A - Bulb; B - Heart; C - Wizard's Hat.
   ii) N - Horizontal Shaded Fill; O - Lattice Shaded Fill.
8) **c**
   i) R - No Line; S - Horizontal Line; T - Vertical Line.
   ii) F - Large Square; G - Small Square.
9) **d**
   i) F - Large Cross Shapes; G - Small Cross Shapes.
   ii) L - Square with Black Fill; M - Square with White Fill; N - No Square.

© 2006 Stephen Curran

11+ Non-verbal Reasoning
Year 5-7 Workbook 2

Answers

10) **a**
   i) W, X, Y, Z - Four Helmet Shapes rotated differently.
   ii) A - Circle with Black Fill; B - Circle with White Fill.

Exercise 8: 2
1) **d**
   i) Fills: A - White, Black, White; B - 1 Black, 2 White; C - 2 White, 1 Black.
   ii) S - Pentagon; T - Triangle.
2) **c**
   i) Square position: X - Bottom; Y - Top; Z - Middle.
   ii) Rectangle fills: K - White; L - Horizontal Shaded.
3) **a**
   i) P - White Fill; Q - Left Slant Shaded Fill.
   ii) Semi-circle position: F - Middle; G - Bottom; H - Top.
4) **e**
   i) S - Black Fills; T - White Fills.
   ii) Star positions: X - Left Slant; Y - Right Slant; Z - Vertical.
5) **e**
   i) R - Solid Line; S - Dashed Line.
   ii) Circle position: J - Top right; K - Bottom left; L - Bottom right.
6) **b**
   i) L - Circle; M - Square.
   ii) Fill type: C - Black; D - Right Slant Shaded; E - White.
7) **e**
   i) Shaded fill type: F - Horizontal; G - Vertical; H - Right Slant.
   ii) X - Ellipse; Y - Octagon; Z - Quadrant.
8) **a**
   i) Line type: A - Vertical; B - Horizontal; C - Diagonal.
   ii) Square type: P - Small; Q - Large; R - Medium.
9) **b**
   i) Quadrant fill: R - Bottom right; S - Top left; T - Bottom left; U - Top right.
   ii) Fill type: N - Speckled; O - Black; P - Left Slant Shaded.

10) **c**
   i) Shape positions: A - Right Slant; B - Vertical; C - Left Slant.
   ii) Fill order: L - 2 White, 1 Black; M - 1 Black, 2 White; N - White, Black, White.

Exercise 8: 3
1) **c**
   i) R - Large Ellipse; S - Small Ellipse.
   ii) Enclosed Ellipse: M - White Fill; N - Black Fill.
   iii) Large Ellipse: A - White Fill; B - Vertical Fill; C - Horizontal Fill.
2) **e**
   i) A - Triangle; B - Square.
   ii) Circles: L - White Fill; M - Black Fill.
   iii) S - Solid Line; T - Dashed Line.
3) **a**
   i) X - Small Pentagon; Y - Small Circle.
   ii) K - Not enclosed; L - Enclosed shapes.
   iii) P - Black Fill; R - White Fill.
4) **e**
   i) G - Speaker faces left; H - Speaker faces right.
   ii) Y - Rectangle Horizontal; Z - Rectangle Vertical.
   iii) R - Black Fills; S - White Fills.
5) **d**
   i) W - Black Fill; X - White Fill.
   ii) M - Small Triangle; N - Large Triangle.
   iii) J - Large Circle; K - Small Circle.
6) **a**
   i) Q - House or Pentagon; R - Shield; S - Flag or Ribbon.
   ii) Arrow direction: G - Points right; F - Points up.
   iii) A - Black Fill; B - Grey Fill.
7) **e**
   i) L - Stars horizontal; M - Stars vertical.
   ii) Fills: Q - 2 Black, 1 White; P - 3 Black; O - 2 White, 1 Black.
   iii) Y - Circle; Z - Hexagon.
8) **b**
   i) T - Octagon; U - Square; V - Circle.
   ii) Enclosed shapes: A - Flower; B - Cross; C - Bulb.
   iii) Q - White Fill; R - Speckled Fill.

Answers

11+ Non-verbal Reasoning Year 5-7 Workbook 2

9) **d**
 i) Star Direction: G - Points up; H - Points down.
 ii) L - Shaded Fill; M - White Fill.
 iii) A - Star split into three sections; B - Star split into four sections.
10) **b**
 i) J - Large Shield; K - Small Shield.
 ii) Shield fills: Q - Squares; P - White.
 iii) Flower fills: Y - White; Z - Black.

Exercise 8: 4

1) **e**
 i) E - Square; F - Circle.
 ii) M - Black Fill; N - White Fill.
 iii) A - Shape at bottom; B - Shape to left; C - Shape to right.
 iv) P - Arrow Ending; Q - Straight Ending.
2) **b**
 i) Z - Thick Line; X - Thin Line.
 ii) L - 2 Circles with Black Fill; M - No Circles with Black Fill.
 iii) P - 4 Circles with Grey Fill or 7 Circles in total; Q - 3 Circles with Grey Fill or 6 Circles in total.
 iv) C - Shape upright; D - Shape faces left; E - Shape faces down.
3) **b**
 i) X - Circle with Black Fill; Y - Circle with White Fill.
 ii) K - Enclosed shape with Grey Fill; L - Enclosed shape with Cross-hatch Fill.
 iii) P - Enclosed Bean Shape; Q - Enclosed Shield Shape; R - Enclosed Helmet Shape.
 iv) C - Enclosed Square with Black Fill; D - Enclosed Square with White Fill.
4) **c**
 i) G - Square with Grey Fill; H - Square with White Fill.
 ii) Y - Circle with Black Fill; Z - No Circle.
 iii) R - Horizontal/Vertical Lines; S - Horizontal Line; T - Vertical Line.
 iv) J - Star with White Fill; K - Star with Black Fill.

5) **a**
 i) W - Cross Shape; X - Star Shape.
 ii) M - Large Shape; N - Small Shape.
 iii) J - Black Fill; K - Vertical Shaded Fill; L - White Fill.
 iv) A - Single shape; B - 2 shapes with overlay.
6) **e**
 i) Q - Square Shape; R - Circle Shape; S - Rectangle Shape.
 ii) G - 2 Segment Shapes with Grey Fill; H - 1 Segment Shape with Grey Fill.
 iii) A - 2 Segment Shapes with White Fill; B - 1 Segment Shape with White Fill.
 iv) W - No shaded Segment Shape; X - 1 Left-Slant Shaded Segment Shape.
7) **d**
 i) K - 2 Cross Shapes; L - 3 Cross Shapes.
 ii) P - Black Fill left of Square; Q - Black Fill bottom of Square.
 iii) X - Triangle upright; Y - Triangle faces down; Z - Triangle faces left.
 iv) D - Thick Line; E - Thin Line.
8) **a**
 i) T - Square on horizontal base; U - Square at diagonal.
 ii) A - Black Fill; B - Grey Fill.
 iii) P - Arrow faces right; Q - Arrow faces up; R - Arrow faces down.
 iv) Y - Grey Border encloses; Z - White Border encloses.
9) **c**
 i) J - Arrow points up; K - Arrow points right.
 ii) Enclosed Arrow: P - White Fill; Q - Black Fill.
 iii) F - Black Fill; G - Grey Fill; H - White Fill in main Arrow Shape.
 iv) Enclosed Arrow: C - Points up; D - Points down.
10) **b**
 i) A - Rectangle with Grey Fill; B - Rectangle with Black Fill.

© 2006 Stephen Curran

11+ Non-verbal Reasoning
Year 5-7 Workbook 2

Answers

ii) F - Rectangle vertical;
G - Rectangle diagonal;
H - Rectangle horizontal.
iii) S - Cross Shape; T - No Cross Shape.
iv) Y - No Square;
Z - Square with Grey Fill encloses Circle.

Chapter Nine
Analogies
Exercise 9: 1
1) **b** - The shape rotates 180°.
2) **a** - Part of the figure transposes vertically (slots together).
3) **b** - The small linked shapes reflect or rotate 180°.
4) **e** - One half of each shape is subtracted.
5) **d** - The lines reverse: Dashed changes to Solid and Solid changes to Dashed.
6) **c** - Half of the Lines of each enclosed shape are subtracted.
7) **a** - The same part of the figure is subtracted (it now has a vertical line of symmetry).
8) **e** - The shape is rotated 180°.
9) **b** - The Heart Shape changes to an Arrow Shape with the same type of line.
10) **c** - The fills reverse: Black changes to White and White changes to Black.

Exercise 9: 2
1) **b**
   i) The shape is rotated 90° anticlockwise.
   ii) The same shape with the fills reversed is added.
2) **c**
   i) An identical shape rotated 90° is added.
   ii) The two shapes merge.
3) **a**
   i) The original shape is enclosed by a larger version of the same shape.
   ii) The Solid Lines of the enclosed shape become Dashed.
4) **d**
   i) The figure rotates 90°.
   ii) The figure reduces.
5) **b**
   i) The figure reflects or rotates 180°.
   ii) The lines reverse: Dashed changes to Solid and Solid changes to Dashed.
6) **e**
   i) The fills reverse: White changes to Shaded and Shaded changes to White.
   ii) The figure enlarges.
7) **d**
   i) The figure flips or inverts vertically.
   ii) An enclosed shape of the same type and rotation is added.
8) **c**
   i) The lines of the outer shape change from Solid to Dashed.
   ii) The figure rotates 90° anticlockwise.
9) **a**
   i) The White Fill changes to a Right Slant Shaded Fill.
   ii) The shape is enclosed by a same type shape with Dashed Lines.
10) **b**
   i) The main shape is vertically inverted or flipped.
   ii) The small shape is vertically transposed.

Exercise 9: 3
1) **e**
   i) The figure reduces.
   ii) The figure rotates 45° anticlockwise.
   iii) The same shape with a Black Fill is added above the first shape.
2) **a**
   i) The outer line of the figure becomes thicker.
   ii) The figure rotates 90°.
   iii) The shape that overlays becomes enclosed.
3) **c**
   i) The fill changes from White to Lattice.
   ii) The sides of the enclosed shape double in number.
   iii) The shape is enclosed by a Circle with a Grey Fill.

© 2006 Stephen Curran

Answers

11+ Non-verbal Reasoning
Year 5-7 Workbook 2

4) **b**
   i) The figure rotates 90° anticlockwise.
   ii) The fills reverse: Black changes to White and White changes to Black.
   iii) The shape enlarges.

5) **d**
   i) The outer shape is subtracted.
   ii) The enclosed shape rotates 180°.
   iii) The Line in the enclosed shape is subtracted.

6) **e**
   i) The figure vertically inverts or flips.
   ii) The Line of the outer shape changes from Thick to Thin.
   iii) The Lines in the enclosed shape change from Solid to Dotted.

7) **b**
   i) The ends of the overlay shape are subtracted leaving an enclosure.
   ii) Two of the enclosed fills swap: Grey changes to White and White changes to Grey.
   iii) Right Slant Shading is added to the outer shape.

8) **e**
   i) The outer shape transposes (moves closer to the main shape).
   ii) The Lines change from Solid to Dashed.
   iii) One shape becomes an overlay.

9) **e**
   i) The second figure rotates 90° clockwise.
   ii) The fills change in the second figure: Right Slant changes to Left Slant Shaded.
   iii) The first figure's fills reverse: White changes to Shaded and Shaded changes to White.

10) **b**
   i) The outer shape on the left rotates 180° or flips vertically.
   ii) The outer shapes transpose horizontally and overlay the main shape.
   iii) A Grey Fill is added to the shape on the left.

Exercise 9: 4

1) **e**
   i) The figure rotates 90° anticlockwise.
   ii) A Dashed Line is added across the middle of the figure.
   iii) The two enclosed shapes swap places (transpose).
   iv) An Ellipse with a Grey Fill is added to the outside of the figure.

2) **b**
   i) The figure rotates 90°.
   ii) The two outer parts of the figure transpose and join together.
   iii) The original shape is enclosed by a new outer shape.
   iv) The ends of part of the enclosed shape have been subtracted.

3) **a**
   i) The figure rotates 90° anticlockwise.
   ii) The same outer shape, rotated at 180° or vertically inverted, is added.
   iii) The two shapes merge.
   iv) A Circle fill changes from Black to White.

4) **d**
   i) The Circle fill changes from White to Right Slant Shading.
   ii) The Square fill changes from White to Black.
   iii) The other half of the outer shape is added.
   iv) The two shapes are enclosed by the outer shape.

5) **b**
   i) The figure rotates 90° clockwise.
   ii) The non-letter shapes swap positions (transpose).
   iii) One shape changes from a White Fill to a Grey Fill.
   iv) The letter is replaced by the next letter in the alphabet.

6) **d**
   i) The Lines of one shape in the figure change from Solid to Dashed.
   ii) One shape in the figure vertically inverts or flips.

11+ Non-verbal Reasoning
Year 5-7 Workbook 2

Answers

iii) One shape in the figure reflects or flips horizontally.
iv) Part of the joining Line is subtracted (made shorter).
7) **c**
 i) The figure rotates 90°.
 ii) The Dotted Line changes to Solid in the central shape.
 iii) The fill in the central shape changes from White to Left Slant Shaded.
 iv) The two outer shapes transpose and join together.
 v) The figure is enclosed by an additional outer shape.
8) **b**
 i) The figure vertically inverts/flips or rotates 180°.
 ii) An outer shape encloses the original figure.
 iii) The Lines of the enclosed shape change from Solid to Dashed.
 iv) A Square is added above the figure.
9) **d**
 i) The figure rotates 90° clockwise.
 ii) A White Fill Square is added.
 iii) The smaller Circle transposes and is enclosed within the Set Square Shape.
 iv) The small Circle rotates a further 90° clockwise.
 v) A Grey Fill is added to the larger Circle.
10) **e**
 i) The shape rotates 180°.
 ii) The shape enlarges.
 iii) The shape is enclosed by a new outer shape of the same type.
 iv) A Star Shape is added below the figure.

Chapter Ten
Similarities
Exercise 10: 1
1) **d** - There must be no Straight Lines.
2) **c** - The shape must have a Square Ending.
3) **e** - The shape must be a Triangle.
4) **d** - The shape must have a fill with Right Slant Shading.
5) **a** - The outer shape must only enclose a Five-pointed Star Shape.
6) **a** - The shape must be a Quadrilateral.
7) **e** - The outer shape must enclose a Circle with a Grey Fill.
8) **c** - The shape must be an Arrow with a Grey Fill.
9) **b** - The figure must have two Straight Sides or both Curved and Straight Sides.
10) **c** - The figure must have Vertical or Horizontal Shading.

Exercise 10: 2
1) **d**
 i) The shapes must be of different sizes.
 ii) The fills: two largest shapes - Black; smallest - White.
2) **b**
 i) One figure is rotated 90° to the other figure.
 ii) The fills reverse: Black changes to White and White changes to Black.
3) **c**
 i) Two of the shapes must be linked.
 ii) Two of the shapes must merge.
4) **d**
 i) Enclosed shapes always stay the same size.
 ii) The outer shape has an odd number of sides.
5) **e**
 i) A linked Square occurs on every vertex.
 ii) The shape is split into two by a Dashed Line.
6) **b**
 i) There must be four Octagons.
 ii) There must be one Cross Shape.
7) **a**
 i) The enclosed Pentagon fills: 1 White; 2 Black.
 ii) The Dashed Line must be of the correct type.

Answers

11+ Non-verbal Reasoning
Year 5-7 Workbook 2

8) **c**
   i) The main figure (excluding the enclosure) must be the same.
   ii) The enclosed shape must be a Wave or a Fish.
9) **c**
   i) The figure must have a vertical line of symmetry.
   ii) The outer shape must have a Thick Solid Line.
10) **d**
   i) The Dotted Line must run from one vertex to another vertex.
   ii) The Dotted Line must be a line of symmetry.

Exercise 10: 3
1) **e**
   i) The shape is in two halves: Shaded and White Fill.
   ii) The shading is perpendicular to the centre line.
   iii) The shape must rest on a horizontal base.
2) **b**
   i) The outer shape must have a Dashed Line.
   ii) The three enclosed shapes must be in the same order.
   iii) There can only be three enclosed shapes.
3) **c**
   i) The Lines of the main Rectangle halve each smaller shape.
   ii) The fills in size order must be White, Black, White.
   iii) Only one small shape can lie on any one side of the main Rectangle.
4) **a**
   i) The larger shape overlays the Squares.
   ii) The enclosed and outer shape are the same rotation.
   iii) The Squares must only occur at the vertices.
5) **b**
   i) Four Lines must cross the shape.
   ii) The two enclosed Squares must have different fills.

iii) The enclosed shapes must be a Circle and a Square, or two Squares.
6) **d**
   i) The Arrow Shapes must be of the same size.
   ii) Both Arrow Shapes must point clockwise.
   iii) Mergers occur at the end of one, and in the middle of the other Arrow Shape.
7) **a**
   i) Two shapes must be of the same size and one must be smaller.
   ii) There must only be two linkages.
   iii) All three shapes must be of the same type.
8) **e**
   i) The two shapes must be of different sizes.
   ii) One shape must overlay the other shape.
   iii) Both shapes in the figure must be of the same rotation.
9) **c**
   i) One shape is rotated 90° to the other shape.
   ii) One shape has Dotted Lines and the other has Solid Lines.
   iii) A Solid Horizontal Line must cross the Solid Line Shape.
10) **d**
   i) The three shapes must be the same type.
   ii) The three shapes must be of different sizes.
   iii) There must be a White, Grey and a Right Slant Shaded Fill.

Exercise 10: 4
1) **c**
   i) One large shape has one more side than the other.
   ii) The two large shapes are linked.
   iii) Each large shape has an enclosure.
   iv) One enclosed shape must have a Black Fill.
2) **d**
   i) The Arrow Shape points to the right.
   ii) The enclosed Ellipse slants to the right.
   iii) A White Fill Square is enclosed by an Ellipse.
   iv) The Ellipse is always the same size.

© 2006 Stephen Curran

11+ Non-verbal Reasoning
Year 5-7 Workbook 2

Answers

3) **b**
  i) One enclosed shape is a smaller version of the outer shape.
  ii) The enclosed Heart Shape must have a White or Black Fill.
  iii) The Cross Shape must not be rotated.
  iv) The three enclosed shapes must be in the same position.
4) **d**
  i) Either the Triangle or Star Shape has a line of symmetry drawn on.
  ii) All the shapes have sides of equal length.
  iii) The shapes can only be Stars, Triangles or Squares.
  iv) One shape must have a Black Fill.
5) **b**
  i) The main shape must be a Quadrilateral.
  ii) The shape must be divided in half by a Line.
  iii) The shading must not be parallel to the Line.
  iv) The main shape overlays an Ellipse with a Grey Fill.
6) **b**
  i) The two outer shapes must be the same.
  ii) One outer shape has a Thick Line and the other a Thin Line.
  iii) Enclosed shapes have one less side than outer shapes.
  iv) One outer shape has a Grey Fill and the other a White Fill.
7) **d**
  i) The enclosed shapes within the Pentagon must be different.
  ii) The number of enclosed and surrounding shapes match.
  iii) Within the Pentagon, one shape must have a Black Fill.
  iv) Outside the Pentagon, one shape must have a Grey Fill.
8) **a**
  i) The medium sized shape overlays the small shape.
  ii) The shapes must not be rotated.
  iii) Shaded and block fills must alternate.
  iv) The shaded fills must be horizontal.

9) **c**
  i) The figure must have one linkage and one merger.
  ii) The Hexagons must be different sizes.
  iii) The enclosed shape fills: 1 Black; 1 White.
  iv) The two enclosed shapes must be Squares.
  v) All the large shapes are Hexagons.
10) **d**
  i) One figure is rotated 180° in relation to the other.
  ii) The Square fill is half Black and half White.
  iii) The Circles must have Grey Fills.
  iv) The figures are offset (transposed) in relation to each other.
  v) One outer shape has a Solid Line and the other a Dashed Line.

Chapter Eleven
Series
Exercise 11: 1
1) **b**
The figure rotates 90° anticlockwise at each stage; Repetitive.
2) **c**
The Shaded Octagon rotates clockwise at each stage; Repetitive.
3) **b**
One Line is added to the Zigzag Shape at each stage; Cumulative.
4) **e**
The figure is rotated anticlockwise by 90° at each stage; Repetitive.
5) **c**
The Cross Shape enlarges and then reduces; Repetitive.
6) **d**
The shape rotates 90° anticlockwise at each stage; Repetitive.
7) **e**
One more shape is added at each stage; Cumulative.
8) **b**
The figure rotates 45° anticlockwise at each stage; Repetitive.

Answers

11+ Non-verbal Reasoning Year 5-7 Workbook 2

9) **d**
The Pentagon and Flower Shapes alternate at each stage; Repetitive.

10) **a**
A change in frequency occurs: shape sides increase by one at each stage; Cumulative.

Exercise 11: 2

1) **e**
  i) The Square with a Grey Fill rotates clockwise around the figure.
  ii) A quarter of the Circle is added at each stage in an anticlockwise direction.

2) **c**
  i) The figure rotates 45° at each stage.
  ii) The fill overlay alternates between Grey and Black at each stage.

3) **a**
  i) One Pentagon transposes clockwise within the Square.
  ii) The linkage fill alternates between Black and Grey.

4) **e**
  i) One Line moves from right to left at each stage.
  ii) One Square fill changes from Black to White at each stage and then back to Black again.

5) **a**
  i) The figure rotates 180° at each stage.
  ii) The fills alternate between Black and White in the Arrow and enclosed Star.

6) **c**
  i) The overlay shapes alternate in position: middle shape; two outer shapes, etc.
  ii) The fill positions swap at each stage: Shaded changes to White and White changes to Shaded, etc.

7) **b**
  i) The Segment Shapes on the left transpose vertically at each stage.
  ii) The right-hand side of the Black Fill Shape transposes vertically at each stage.

8) **d**
  i) The figure reflects, then vertically flips or inverts, then reflects, etc.
  ii) The background fills alternate between Grey and White at each stage.

9) **c**
  i) The figure rotates clockwise 90°.
  ii) The Square fill pattern changes from White to Grey to Black, etc.

10) **a**
  i) The Black Fill moves towards the outside of the shape and back again at each stage.
  ii) The Cross Shape alternates between the two types at each stage.

Exercise 11: 3

1) **c**
  i) The Circles must have a Grey Fill.
  ii) The size sequence for the three central shapes is large, medium, small, etc.
  iii) The Arrow rotates around the Square in an anticlockwise direction.

2) **d**
  i) The Circle frequency alternates between two and four.
  ii) The Dashed Lines from the previous figure become Solid.
  iii) Two Dashed Lines are added at each stage to build the Cross Shape.

3) **a**
  i) A small Square is enclosed, then enlarges to enclose a new shape, etc.
  ii) A new shape is introduced for two stages only.
  iii) The shape fills reverse at each stage: Black changes to White and White changes to Black.

4) **b**
  i) The figure rotates 90° clockwise at each stage.
  ii) The Square fills alternate between Black and White at each stage.
  iii) A Diagonal Line is added at each stage.

5) **c**
  i) Ellipses are rotated 90° anticlockwise alternately.
  ii) Ellipses are transformed: stretched at every other stage.

© 2006 Stephen Curran

11+ Non-verbal Reasoning
Year 5-7 Workbook 2

Answers

iii) Ellipse fills alternate between Black and Grey at every other stage.
6) **c**
  i) A Square with a Black Fill is added at each stage to the Arrow Shape with a White Fill.
  ii) A Black Arrow Shape is added at each stage.
  iii) All the Arrow Shapes change direction at each stage.
7) **a**
  i) The Cigar Shape Lines alternate between Dashed and Solid at each stage.
  ii) A Line is added to the top, then the bottom, then the top, etc.
  iii) A Square with a Black Fill is added to the bottom, then the top, then the bottom, etc.
8) **b**
  i) The figure rotates anticlockwise.
  ii) A Circle with a Black Fill is added at each stage.
  iii) A Line is added at each stage.
9) **e**
  i) The whole figure rotates 90°.
  ii) The Bulb Shape rotates a further 180°.
  iii) The fills change from Horizontal Shaded to Cross-hatched Squares to Vertical Shaded, etc.
10) **b**
  i) The figure reflects (Squares alternate between Left Slant and Right Slant).
  ii) A Line is added at each stage.
  iii) The Squares fill pattern: Black changes to White; White changes to Black (same at every other stage).

Exercise 11: 4
1) **b**
  i) One Cross Shape is added at each stage.
  ii) One Square with a White Fill is added at each stage.
  iii) One Hexagon is added at each stage.
  iv) The Hexagon fill alternates Black, White, Black, White, etc.
2) **c**
  i) The Speaker Shape rotates 90° anticlockwise.

ii) The Circle fill alternates White, Black, White, etc.
iii) The Circle rotates around the Speaker Shape in an anticlockwise direction.
iv) The shading alternates Left Slant, Horizontal, Left Slant, Horizontal, etc.
3) **d**
  i) A Line is subtracted from the Cross Shape at each stage.
  ii) A Quadrant Shape is subtracted from the corner in an anticlockwise direction.
  iii) A Curved Line is added each time to build the Circle.
  iv) A Semi-circle is added to the side in an anticlockwise direction at each stage.
4) **c**
  i) The Quadrant Shape with a Block Fill alternates between Black and Grey.
  ii) The Black/Grey Fill Quadrant Shape rotates 180° at each stage.
  iii) The Shaded Quadrant Shape rotates 90° in a clockwise direction.
  iv) Every other figure is an enclosed Quadrant with a White Fill.
5) **d**
  i) The Circle fill alternates Black, White, Black, etc.
  ii) The repetitive pattern for all the shapes is 3, 3, 2, 2, 1, 1, 0, 0, 3, 3, etc.
  iii) The Triangles rotate 180° at each stage.
  iv) Square fills alternate Grey, White, Grey, etc.
6) **b**
  i) The Chevron Shapes rotate 90° clockwise at each stage.
  ii) The cumulative pattern for the Chevron Shapes is 2, 2, 3, 3, 4, 4, etc.
  iii) The cumulative pattern for the Circles is 1, 1, 2, 2, 3, 3, etc.
  iv) The Circles transpose: alternate between top, bottom, top at each stage.
7) **a**
  i) A Square is added at each stage.
  ii) The first Circle must have a White Fill.
  iii) A Circle is added at each stage.
  iv) The outer Squares must have White Fills.

© 2006 Stephen Curran

Answers

11+ Non-verbal Reasoning Year 5-7 Workbook 2

8) **e**
  i) Shapes rotate in a clockwise direction around the Square.
  ii) A Pentagon with a White Fill is replaced by a Cross Shape with a Black Fill at each stage.
  iii) A Pentagon with a Grey Fill is added at each stage.
  iv) A Cross Shape with a White Fill is subtracted at each stage.

9) **c**
  i) The Arrow Shape rotates 180° at each stage.
  ii) The Cross Shapes transpose horizontally and vertically at each stage.
  iii) A Cross Shape is added at each stage.
  iv) An Arrowhead is added at each stage.
  v) A Line is added to the bottom of the Arrow Shape at each stage.

10) **d**
  i) The figures are grouped in pairs.
  ii) The outer shape rotates 90° clockwise in its pairing.
  iii) A Circle with a Grey Fill is added and enclosed by the outer shape.
  iv) The larger enclosed shape reflects.
  v) Fills reverse: the larger shape changes to Shaded and the larger enclosed shape changes to White.

Chapter Twelve
Matrices
Exercise 12: 1

1) **c**
Horizontal: The fill changes from White to Vertical Shaded **or** Vertical: The Heptagon becomes a Square.

2) **a**
Horizontal: The shape rotates 90° anticlockwise.

3) **b**
Horizontal: The shape reduces and keeps its fill.

4) **b**
Horizontal and Vertical: There is one of each type of shape **or** Left Diagonal: The shapes are the same.

5) **c**
Horizontal and vertical: The shape types alternate **or** Left and Right Diagonal: The shapes are the same in each Diagonal.

6) **c**
Vertical: The figure reflects in a vertical direction or rotates 180° **or** Horizontal: There is one of each type of figure.

7) **e**
Horizontal: A vertical line of reflective symmetry can be drawn through the middle of the matrix.

8) **d**
Vertical: A horizontal line of reflective symmetry can be drawn across the middle of the matrix.

9) **c**
Diagonal: A left or right diagonal line of reflective symmetry can be drawn through the matrix.

10) **b**
Vertical: The figure rotates 45° **or** Horizontal: There is one of each type of figure.

Exercise 12: 2

1) **a** - Solve vertically.
  i) The whole figure reflects.
  ii) The Dotted Line of the enclosed shape changes to Solid.

2) **c** - Solve horizontally.
  i) The outer two shape fills swap: Grey changes to White and White changes to Grey.
  ii) The second largest enclosed shape fill changes from Black to White.

3) **e** - Solve vertically.
  i) One enclosure is created by a Square, followed by a Circle.
  ii) The outer shape in each column must have one of each fill.

4) **d** - Solve vertically.
  i) The shape reflects.
  ii) The Solid Lines become Dashed and Dashed Lines become Solid.

5) **e** - Solve vertically.
  i) The figure reflects.
  ii) The fills reverse.

11+ Non-verbal Reasoning
Year 5-7 Workbook 2

Answers

6) **d** - This matrix can be solved in either direction.
   i) There is one of each shape horizontally and vertically.
   ii) The size pattern: three sizes vertically; same size horizontally.
7) **c** - Solve vertically.
   i) The figure reflects (or rotates 180°).
   ii) The Square fill changes from White to Black.
8) **b** - Solve horizontally.
   i) The shapes enlarge in size from left to right.
   ii) There is one of each fill type: Grey, Vertical Shaded, Lattice.
9) **c** - Solve horizontally.
   i) The number of Bars, Circles or Notches is 1, 2, 3 from left to right.
   ii) There are three sizes of each figure: small, medium, large.
10) **e** - Solve horizontally.
    i) The figure reflects.
    ii) The fill of the small shape changes from Black to White.

Exercise 12: 3

1) **d** - Solve horizontally.
   i) Each row has alternating large and small figures.
   ii) Each row has one of each fill type: Grey, White, Shaded.
   iii) Lines across small shapes run the same way as the shading.
2) **e** - Solve vertically.
   i) The whole figure reflects.
   ii) The small figure fills reverse: Grey changes to White and White changes to Grey.
   iii) Half of the large figure is subtracted.
3) **a** - Solve horizontally.
   i) There must be one of each size of shape in each row.
   ii) There must be one of each type of fill: Shaded, Grey, White.
   iii) Pattern of added Lines: 1 Line, 2 Lines, shape enclosure.

4) **c** - Solve horizontally.
   i) The figure vertically inverts or flips.
   ii) One Slanted Line is subtracted.
   iii) The remaining Line becomes thicker.
5) **d** - Solve horizontally.
   i) Each row has Cross Shapes, a line shape and a standard shape.
   ii) Within a row, the figures have the same number of vertices.
   iii) Each row has a Grey, White and Black Fill Circle.
6) **a** - Solve horizontally.
   i) The whole figure rotates 180°.
   ii) The Lines reverse: Solid changes to Dashed and Dashed changes to Solid.
   iii) The enclosed shape is subtracted.
7) **d** - Solve horizontally.
   i) The figure gradually rotates clockwise from left to right.
   ii) The three figures in each row must have 2, 4 or 6 protruding Lines.
   iii) The fills reverse: Black changes to White and White changes to Black.
8) **b** - Solve vertically.
   i) The main shapes are in three positions: bottom, middle, top.
   ii) The Square Ended Shape rotates 90° each stage.
   iii) There is one of each fill pattern: Grey and White; White and Grey; Mixed.
9) **c** - This matrix can be solved in either direction.
   i) The figure rotates 90° each stage.
   ii) There must be one enclosed Cross Shape in every row and column.
   iii) The main shapes are of three line types: Solid, Dashed, Dotted.
10) **b** - Solve vertically.
    i) The top left shape reflects vertically to bottom left.
    ii) The top right shape reflects to top left.
    iii) The bottom left Grey Fill Shape reflects diagonally (or rotates 180°) to top right.

Answers

*11+ Non-verbal Reasoning
Year 5-7 Workbook 2*

Exercise 12: 4

1) **c** - This matrix can be solved in either direction.
   i) Arrow Shapes are rotated 90° by row and 180° by column.
   ii) There is one of each Square fill type by row/column: Black, Grey, White.
   iii) The number of Squares: 1, 2, 3 by column; same number in each row.
   iv) By row/column: The Arrow has 0, 1, 2 extra Lines in any order.

2) **a** - Solve horizontally.
   i) The figure reflects horizontally.
   ii) The central shape fill alternates between Black and White.
   iii) There is a pattern of 1, 2 and 3 Line Shapes in each row.
   iv) The Line Shape sizes change: small, medium, large (left to right).

3) **c** - Solve vertically.
   i) The Cigar Shape and its enclosure reflects or rotates 180°.
   ii) The Rectangle rotates 180° or the fills swap places.
   iii) The Triangle reflects vertically or rotates 180°.
   iv) The fill of the outer part in the Cigar Shape changes from White to Black.

4) **d** - Solve horizontally.
   i) The figure reflects or the Thick Line transposes.
   ii) The Arrow Heads change direction.
   iii) The small Square is subtracted.
   iv) The large Square encloses the remaining small shape.

5) **e** - Solve horizontally.
   i) The Lines reverse: Thick changes to Thin and Thin changes to Thick.
   ii) The Circle transposes, moving to the centre of the figure.
   iii) One small shape enlarges to reflect the large shape.
   iv) The fill in the original large shape changes from White to Grey.

6) **b** - Solve horizontally.
   i) The Line transposes vertically.
   ii) A reflection of the figure (excluding the Triangle) is added.
   iii) The Triangle transposes.
   iv) A Dashed Vertical line of symmetry is added to the figure.

7) **e** - Solve horizontally.
   i) The Black Fill Shape transposes out of the Semi-circle.
   ii) The Semi-circle transposes downwards.
   iii) The smaller shape enlarges and encloses the Semi-circle.
   iv) The Rectangle squashes vertically.

8) **a** - Solve horizontally.
   i) One Square is subtracted.
   ii) The Circle fills change from Black to White.
   iii) One Line is subtracted.
   iv) One Cross Shape is added.

9) **b** - Solve horizontally.
   i) The top shape rotates 90° anticlockwise.
   ii) The bottom shape inverts or flips horizontally.
   iii) The two shapes swap places (transpose vertically).
   iv) The Shaded Fills in the two shapes must be at 90° to each other.

10) **d** - This matrix can be solved in either direction.
    i) There are three different shapes by row and by column.
    ii) The row and column fills: Grey, Lattice, Horizontal Shading.
    iii) The shape sizes: small, medium, large by column; same by row.
    iv) The Arrow Shapes vertically invert by row; Horizontally by column.
    v) The matrix must have three different rotations of each shape.

11+ Non-verbal Reasoning
Year 5-7 Workbook 2

Answers

Chapter Thirteen
Revision
Exercise 13: 1a
1) **a**
2) **b**
3) **c**
4) **b**
5) **e**

Exercise 13: 1b
6) **d**
7) **a**
8) **b**
9) **c**
10) **a**

Exercise 13: 2a
1) **e**
2) **b**
3) **d**
4) **a**
5) **b**

Exercise 13: 2b
6) **c**
7) **a**
8) **c**
9) **d**
10) **b**

Exercise 13: 3a
1) **e**
2) **b**
3) **e**
4) **a**
5) **c**

Exercise 13: 3b
6) **c**
7) **e**
8) **a**
9) **d**
10) **b**

© 2006 Stephen Curran

PROGRESS CHARTS

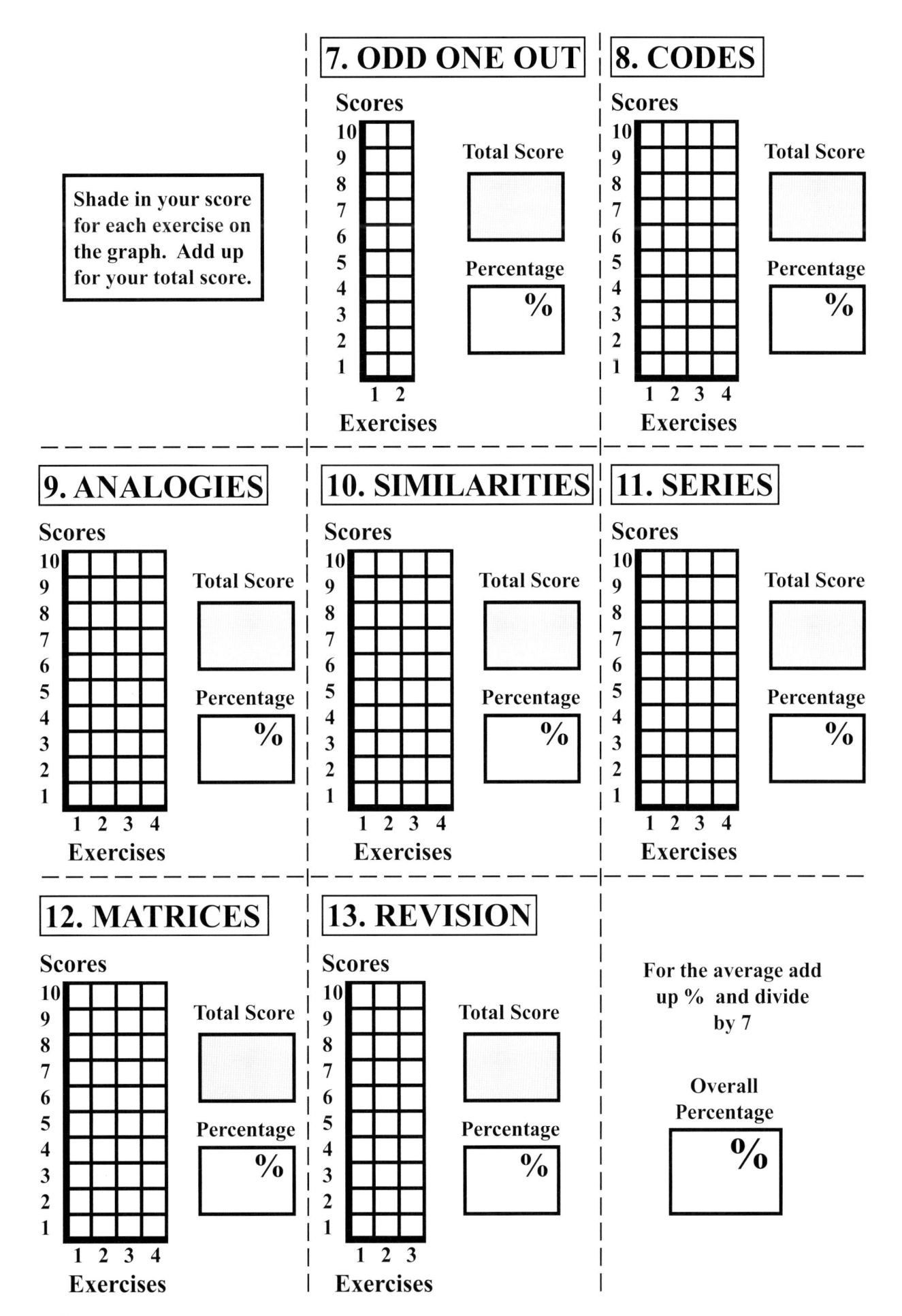

Shade in your score for each exercise on the graph. Add up for your total score.

7. ODD ONE OUT
Scores

Total Score

Percentage %

Exercises 1 2

8. CODES
Scores

Total Score

Percentage %

Exercises 1 2 3 4

9. ANALOGIES
Scores

Total Score

Percentage %

Exercises 1 2 3 4

10. SIMILARITIES
Scores

Total Score

Percentage %

Exercises 1 2 3 4

11. SERIES
Scores

Total Score

Percentage %

Exercises 1 2 3 4

12. MATRICES
Scores

Total Score

Percentage %

Exercises 1 2 3 4

13. REVISION
Scores

Total Score

Percentage %

Exercises 1 2 3

For the average add up % and divide by 7

Overall Percentage %

© 2006 Stephen Curran

CERTIFICATE OF ACHIEVEMENT

This certifies

_____

has successfully completed

11+ Non-verbal Reasoning Year 5–7 WORKBOOK 2

Overall percentage score achieved ☐ %

Comment _____

_____

Signed _____
(teacher/parent/guardian)

Date _____

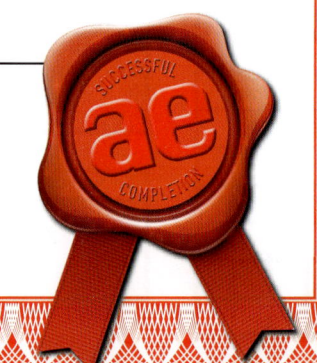